FIRST MOVER

Jeff Bezos In His Own Words

EDITED BY HELENA HUNT

AN AGATE IMPRINT

CHICAGO

Printed in the United States of America

First Mover: Jeff Bezos In His Own Words
ISBN 13: 978-1-57284-243-4
ISBN 10: 1-57284-243-1
eISBN 13: 978-1-57284-813-9
eISBN 10: 1-57284-813-8
First printing: February 2018

10 9 8 7 6 5 4 3 2 1   18 19 20 21 22

B2 Books is an imprint of Agate Publishing. Agate books are available in bulk at discount prices. For more information, go to agatepublishing.com.

FIRST MOVER

"The common question that gets asked in business is, why? That's a good question, but an equally valid question is, why not?"

—JEFF BEZOS

TABLE OF CONTENTS

INTRODUCTION **1**

E-commerce and Amazon.....................................7

Entrepreneurship 29

Business Principles 37

Customer Service 55

Corporate Culture..67

Invention and Innovation..................................77

Technology and Devices.....................................99

Books and Kindle 111

Space and Blue Origin.......................................121

Investments and Philanthropy.......................135

Life Lessons 141

MILESTONES... **153**

INTRODUCTION

T HE ONLINE RETAILER AMAZON MAKES $136 billion in annual revenue as of this writing. If you aren't contributing to Amazon's revenue, perhaps you are making a statement against any number of the company's ethically ambiguous characteristics: its increasingly monopolistic dominance of the e-commerce and retail markets, its often adversarial relationships with book publishers, or its report-edly cold-blooded workplace culture. But Amazon's estimated 65 million Prime members don't seem too worried about these shortcomings. They choose Amazon again and again for its low prices, dedication to customer service, and willingness to expand into new services and product offerings that, in some cases, anticipate customer needs before customers even know they are needs. The word *Amazon* has become synonymous, not with a river in South America, but with a particular ser-vice made possible by the internet—and the vision of Jeff Bezos, Amazon's founder and CEO, to fore-see the possibilities of moving life online.

Bezos would be the first to say that he isn't solely responsible for the success of his $430 billion com-pany and its rapidly multiplying subsidiaries. But it is difficult to imagine the success of Amazon—and ventures such as the *Washington Post* and Blue Origin—without the singular vision, tireless motivation, wide-eyed optimism, and uncanny prescience of the man who started it all.

That prescience is key to most of Bezos's success. In 1994, when he was working at quantitative hedge fund D.E. Shaw in Manhattan, Bezos came across a surprising statistic: the recently created internet was growing at a staggering rate of 2,300 percent a year. Bezos knew he had to join (and, hopefully, monetize) this wave of growth before it left him behind, and so he acted quickly—leaving his job, picking up a Chevy Blazer from his parents in Texas, and driving to Seattle, where he planned to sell books via the internet out of his new house's garage. He chose Seattle because it was a large city with a major airport and because it was near a book warehouse in Oregon. He chose to sell books because they were sortable, packable, and shippable—and because a vast selection already existed that couldn't be sold by any single physical retail competitor. In every instance, Bezos applied a keen, almost cold, talent for analysis, optimization, and rapid movement that has proven to serve him well.

Now, more than 20 years later, Amazon will sell you almost anything. You can buy tents, tires, Barbie dolls, fresh food, and restaurant meals on the website, as well as on the devices Amazon itself has pioneered—most significantly, the Kindle, the first dedicated e-reader, and the Echo, an artificially intelligent, voice-activated, multiuse home device. The company's stock price has soared, and Bezos himself is worth billions of dollars.

The success of Amazon didn't always seem so certain, however. In the late 1990s and early 2000s, during the dot-com boom and bust, analysts called Bezos's company "Amazon.bomb," "Amazon.con," and "Amazon.toast." Bezos's business plan was to have razor-thin margins, relentlessly cutting costs to draw customers while at the same time expanding fulfillment capabilities and selection, a strategy that didn't always create profits or appeal to investors. As stock prices fell, Bezos held on to the mission of Amazon: to be Earth's most customer-centric company. He took the long view, and despite warnings and analysts' predictions, he did what it took to serve his customers—and that included staying in business.

Bezos believes that his customer-forward business model—predict what people need before they realize they need it—is really what drives innovation. This philosophy led to Amazon, of course, but also to Amazon Web Services, a data infrastructure that developers and services such as Netflix, Spotify, and the CIA rent from Amazon; Kindle, an e-reader that Bezos claims improves the technology of the book; and even Blue Origin, Bezos's space company, which also has a forward-thinking, customer-obsessed mentality.

Someday, Bezos reasons, people will need to go to space; we might as well start building them a service to do that now.

While the customer-centric model may have won over Amazon's vast membership, for employees it can create a punishing environment that isn't oriented to their wants or needs. The infamous 2015 *New York Times* profile "Inside Amazon: Wrestling Big Ideas in a Bruising Workplace" describes a corporate culture where employees cry at their desks, are encouraged to leave if they face pregnancy or illness, and struggle against cutthroat internal competition. *The Everything Store*, a nonfiction account of Amazon's rise by Brad Stone, quotes Bezos asking employees "Are you lazy or just incompetent?" and "Do I need to go down and get the certificate that says I'm CEO of the company to get you to stop challenging me on this?" among other choice phrases.

In public, Bezos may not be as openly confrontational, but he does explain that his company thrives on constant invention, and those who can't keep up will be left behind—whether they're inside or outside Amazon. But in many ways Bezos still seems to be the earnest intellectual whom a 1999 *60 Minutes* segment dubbed "Nerd of the Amazon." He started Blue Origin in part because he was a fan of *Star Trek* (a *Star Trek* game on the school computer was what first got him interested in computers, too). His determination to go to space goes at least as far back as his high school valedictory speech, where he described building hotels and amusement parks for space colonists.

Bezos has followed his passions to a remarkable level of success. Because he's already accomplished so much that once seemed so unlikely, it's hard not to believe him now when he describes a future where millions of people live and work in space. And if he has it his way—which he so often does—Jeff Bezos will be among the first to go there.

E-COMMERCE AND AMAZON

••

Original Job Posting

Well-capitalized start-up seeks extremely talented C/C++/Unix developers to help pioneer commerce on the Internet. You must have experience designing and building large and complex (yet maintainable) systems, and you should be able to do so in about one-third the time that most competent people think possible.

—Usenet job posting, August 22, 1994

••

Naming Amazon

Earth's biggest river. Earth's biggest selection. It had nothing to do with single-breasted female warriors.

—92nd Street Y in New York City, April 11, 2001

••

The Internet's Rapid Growth

When something's growing 2,300 percent per year, you have to move fast. A sense of urgency becomes your most valuable asset.

—A.B. Dick Lecture on Entrepreneurship, March 21, 1998

The Garage

I have to admit, we wanted a garage in part because we wanted some of that garage start-up legitimacy.

—Association of American Publishers, March 18, 1999

The First Distribution Center

One of the developers, the day before we opened, as we were looking at this space, said, "I can't figure out if this is incredibly optimistic or hopelessly pathetic." And that was truly how we felt. We just didn't know.

—Association of American Publishers, March 18, 1999

Amazon Began on Its Hands and Knees

We had not planned perfectly. We didn't even have packing tables in this little 400-square-foot warehouse. This was all done on our hands and knees on a cement floor.

—A.B. Dick Lecture on Entrepreneurship, March 21, 1998

The Internet's Gifts

There are a lot of things the internet takes away. But then it also brings gifts, and you have to lean into the gifts.

—The Future of Newspapers, June 21, 2017

What Customers Want

There are three things that are important to our customers: selection, ease of use and convenience, and price. And so every day we work on making sure that each of those three things are better at Amazon.com than they are anywhere else.

—A.B. Dick Lecture on Entrepreneurship,
March 21, 1998

The Value Proposition of the Internet

Being able to do something online that you can't do in any other way is important. It's all about the fundamental tenet of building any business, which is creating a value proposition for the customer.

—A.B. Dick Lecture on Entrepreneurship,
March 21, 1998

• •

Building a Lasting Company

The most frustrating part of shopping is not being able to find what you are looking for. Two years ago, we realized that if we could solve that problem and provide truly universal selection, we could build an important and lasting company.

—*New York Times*, November 28, 1999

• •

Personalization

Discovery is different from finding—finding is you know what you want, you type it into the search engine and we find it for you. Discovery is more about personalization, listmania—all the things that we've done.

—*Guardian*, October 14, 2002

Personalization is like retreating to the time when you have small-town merchants who got to know you, and they could help you get the right products. The right products can improve your life, and the wrong products detract from it. Before the era of mass merchandising, it used to be that most things were personalized.

—*Washington Post*, November 8, 1998

Helping Products Find Customers

When you have so many items, you have to work hard to build tools that help customers find products. But you also have to work hard at something which is a little less intuitive and actually a little—technically a little more challenging—which is to help products find customers.

—lecture to the MIT ACM/IEEE Club,
November 25, 2002

Consumerism at Its Worst

What consumerism really is, at its worst, is getting people to buy things that don't actually improve their lives. The one thing that offends me the most is when I walk by a bank and see ads trying to convince people to take out second mortgages on their home so they can go on vacation. That's approaching evil.

—*Wired*, March 1, 1999

• •

Word of Mouth on the Internet

In the first 30 days, we got orders from all 50 states and 45 different countries, with not a dollar of advertising, just all word of mouth.

—lecture to the MIT ACM/IEEE Club,
November 25, 2002

If you make a customer unhappy on the internet, they won't tell five friends. They will tell 5,000 friends. . . . Likewise, of course, if you can make a customer happy by meeting or exceeding their expectations, they can also tell 5,000 people and be evangelists for you. They can use the internet as a megaphone. . . . The balance of power has shifted away from the merchant and toward the consumer.

—A.B. Dick Lecture on Entrepreneurship,
March 21, 1998

• •

Market Leadership

The stronger our market leadership, the more powerful our economic model. Market leadership can translate directly to higher revenue, higher profitability, greater capital velocity, and correspondingly stronger returns on invested capital.

—letter to shareholders, March 30, 1998

• •

First-Mover Advantages

Amazon.com itself has demonstrated that first-mover advantages on the internet are incredibly powerful.

—A.B. Dick Lecture on Entrepreneurship,
March 21, 1998

We don't have any durable, sustainable advantages that, if we just take a break for a while, somebody else can't catch up.

—*Charlie Rose*, April 2, 1999

Our big advantage is and will continue to be that we know more about the business, just because we have been doing it for longer. The gap between us and our competitors, if we execute well, should widen, not narrow.

—*Bloomberg*, July 14, 2002

••

Limitless Selection

When we were still a very small company, we sent an e-mail message to about a thousand randomly selected customers and asked, "Besides the things we sell today, what would you like to see us sell?" The answers came back to that so long-tailed— people said, "Windshield wiper blades for my car," and so on and so on. It was very surprising. It was at that point—this is probably 1998—that we started to realize that perhaps we could sell a very wide selection of things using the methods that we had pioneered.

—*Foreign Affairs*, January/February 2015

We are limitless. We have virtually every product that exists because we are not constrained by physical limitations.

—*Playboy*, February 2000

••

No Guns

We don't want to sell them. There are a lot of things to sell. We'll let other people sell guns.

—*Playboy*, February 2000

No Yard Rakes

There aren't really products that can't be sold online. There are products that can't be sold economically online. We used to sell yard rakes, at a certain point in time, and that was a very bad decision, because with millions of products, you will have a sprinkling of products that can't possibly make money online. They're too bulky and inexpensive. Big products are fine as long as they're expensive, but if you have a cheap big product, that doesn't work. And so yard rakes were the worst.

—Emerging Technology Conference,
September 27, 2006

Competitive Branding

If you look at the real advantage that, say, Barnes & Noble and Borders as companies have over Amazon .com, it's not the fact so much that they are huge companies with $2.5 billion-plus in sales, although that is a major factor. The key advantage they have is that they have such well-established brand names, and brand names are super-important online. So one of our goals has to be to mitigate that advantage they have by trying to build our brand name as well as we can. And we're certainly focused on doing that.

—*Wired*, June 1, 1997

• •

The Online and the Physical Worlds

In my opinion, the e-commerce world and the online world are going to be as richly varied as the physical world.

—*Dallas Morning News*, August 1999

Strip malls are a symbol for marginal, low-experience stores that nobody really wants to go to. Over time, say within ten years, maybe 15 percent of commerce will move online. Will that have a big impact on the physical world? Absolutely. What will that effect be? It will force stores to get better.

—*Playboy*, February 2000

I get asked all the time, "Why don't you leverage your brand name by opening physical stores?" The problem is, we don't know how we would do that better. It's a well-served space. The people who operate physical stores today do an excellent job, and if we were to do that, we would not be improving anything. So that would hurt our brand reputation.

—*Bloomberg Businessweek*, August 1, 2004

Will All Internet Companies Survive?

There will be many winners created online. You know, the right analogy is the Cambrian explosion 550 million years ago. This was when single-celled life exploded into multicelled life, and you saw the greatest rate of speciation ever seen. But it was also the greatest rate of extinction ever seen. And that's exactly what's going to go on here. You know, it makes sense from society's point of view for all these experiments to be done. If you're one of the extinct species, it doesn't feel too good.

—92nd Street Y in New York City, April 11, 2001

The vast majority of the companies being created today won't work, for one reason or another. And that's a possibility for the leaders like Amazon.com as well.

—*Charlie Rose*, April 2, 1999

Every Company Benefits from the Internet

What we see today is that the internet is still thought of as, you know, kind of like a vertical, where it's like: "These are the 'internet companies.'" And that's how you can tell it's early, because every company is benefiting from the internet.

—*Charlie Rose*, November 19, 2007

••

Industries Succeed

Most often, industries succeed. So I can tell you, I think e-commerce is succeeding. And the way we think about it, nobody else has to fail for us to do well.

—*Charlie Rose*, July 28, 2010

••

Putting Attention on the Back End

When many of the dot-com companies went out of business when the internet bubble burst, one of the reasons is they hadn't really put enough attention into their back end. They hadn't put enough attention into what I think some people consider the less glamorous part of the business, which is the picking, packing, and shipping. We did an extensive analysis and found out that customers actually want to receive their products!

—Edison Nation video series, April 2011

••

A Lean Culture

We will work hard to spend wisely and maintain our lean culture. We understand the importance of continually reinforcing a cost-conscious culture, particularly in a business incurring net losses.

—letter to shareholders, March 30, 1998

....

The Economics of Online Retail

Unlike physical-world retailing, which is a variable-cost business, so if you double your sales you double your costs, online retailing is a fixed-cost business, much more so. So when you double your sales, you don't come anywhere near doubling your costs.

—*Charlie Rose*, June 28, 2000

We all know in the physical world that whatever place has the best service can't have the lowest prices. Online, I think that's wrong. I think online, you can have the best service and the lowest prices if you have enough scale.

—*Charlie Rose*, June 28, 2000

....

Earning Money

We do make money. We do a good job in that retail business, but it is earned through—even though it's very low margins—it's earned through a lot of very careful kind of frugality and focus on defect reduction.

—Startup School, April 19, 2008

••

High and Low Margins

There are two types of retailers: those that work hard to raise prices and those that work hard to lower prices. Though both models can be successful, we've decided to relentlessly follow the second model.

—press release, January 22, 2002

We'd rather have a very large customer base and low margins than a smaller customer base and higher margins.

—*Wired*, November 13, 2011

High margins will also cover a lot of sins. It's impossible to be efficient with high margins because you don't need to be, and necessity is the mother of invention.

—AWS re: Invent, November 29, 2012

••

Taking Price Off the Table

Anybody can lower price. We want to take price off the table. We're saying we're going to have as aggressive pricing as anybody out there, and then let people choose based on the higher level of service that we provide.

—*Wired*, June 1, 1997

··

Eliminating Defects

The most expensive thing you can do is make a mistake. We can afford to focus on smaller and smaller defects and eliminate them at their root. That reduces cost, because things just work.

—*Wired*, November 13, 2011

The further a defect travels downstream, the more expensive it becomes to fix.

—AWS re: Invent, November 29, 2012

As we are able to get smarter, as we're able to, you know, figure out how to do things more efficiently, we are going to be returning those cost efficiencies to customers in the form of lower prices.

—Startup School, April 19, 2008

··

Get the CRAP Out

At a certain point we had a kind of housecleaning. We called it "Get the CRAP Out," where CRAP stood for "Can't Realize Any Profit." And we went through our entire catalog of products removing things like yard rakes.

—Emerging Technology Conference,
September 27, 2006

●●●

The Environmental Impact of E-commerce

If you net this out, the environmental impact of the cardboard—which is biodegradable—is much less than the environmental impact from the emissions from taking the 2,000-pound vehicle to pick up the five pounds of stuff.

—Emerging Technology Conference,
September 27, 2006

●●●

Prime Appeal

Amazon Prime members love getting unlimited two-day shipping for free with no minimum order size. Though expensive for the company, Amazon Prime creates a premium experience for customers who join, and as a result we hope they'll purchase more from us in the long term.

—press release, July 26, 2005

●●●

Global Implementation

I expect to take everything that works in any of our geographies and try to get them to work in all our geographies.

—*Hindu*, September 28, 2014

••

Drone Technology and Regulation

The technology is going very well. The regulatory piece is going a little slower than I would have anticipated. That's going to be the long pole in the tent, we always knew that. The FAA has their hands full, I think, trying to figure out how to regulate drones.

—*CBS This Morning*, February 4, 2015

With respect to drone delivery, putting aside the regulatory obstacles is a little bit like asking Mrs. Lincoln, "Other than that, how was the play?"

—Liberty Science Center Genius Gala 4.0,
May 1, 2015

I just went and met with the primary team and saw the 10th- or 11th-generation drone flying around in the cage. It's truly remarkable. It's not just the physical airframe and electric motors and so on. The most interesting part of this is the autopilot and the guidance and control and the machine vision systems that make it all work.

—*Business Insider*, December 13, 2014

· ·

Amazon and Groceries

What's not to love? You order the groceries online and we deliver them to your door. But that's very expensive.

—*60 Minutes*, December 1, 2013

· ·

Acquisition of Whole Foods

Whole Foods Market has been satisfying, delighting and nourishing customers for nearly four decades— they're doing an amazing job and we want that to continue.

—press release, June 16, 2017

· ·

Storytelling at Amazon Studios

One way you can think about TV is you can say, "I want to make something that millions and millions of people are going to watch." If that's your starting point, you paint yourself into a corner and you often end up with homogenized, uninteresting content. If you say, "Let's hire the world's greatest storytellers. Let's encourage them to take risks," then you're going to end up with a remarkable story, and remarkable stories always find an audience.

—*Hollywood Reporter*, July 15, 2015

We keep our Amazon Studios team size very small so that's consistent with not wanting to interfere with the work the storyteller does.

—*Hollywood Reporter*, July 15, 2015

• •

The Reverse Veto

I'm really a reverse-veto person. I would never say no to something the [Amazon Studios] team wanted to do, but I might say yes to something the team didn't want to do. You want there to be multiple ways to get to "yes" because you want to encourage risk-taking.

—*Hollywood Reporter*, July 15, 2015

• •

Crowdsourced Entertainment

We're changing the greenlighting process. Instead of a few studio executives deciding what gets greenlighted . . . we're using what some people would call crowdsourcing.

—*60 Minutes*, December 1, 2013

••

Prime One Way or Another

There's one group of customers who start their membership because of Prime Instant Video, but they're like, "I got this free two-day shipping thing." There's this other group that starts with free shipping. That's still the bigger group, and they're like, "I can get this cool video." All these things work together.

—*New York Times*, June 19, 2014

••

Golden Globes Sell Shoes

From a business point of view for us, we get to monetize that content in a very unusual way, because when we win a Golden Globe, you know, it helps us sell more shoes. And it does that in a very direct way, because if you look at Prime members, they buy more on Amazon than non-Prime members.

—Code Conference, June 1, 2016

● ●

Amazon Deserves to Be Scrutinized

I'm very, very comfortable with all of Amazon's approaches and behaviors, the way we pay taxes. The political positions that we take are focused on our business and I think highly appropriate. . . . I think a company like Amazon also deserves to be scrutinized and examined and criticized, and I have no worries about that.

—The Washington Post's Transformers, May 18, 2016

● ●

Amazon's Opposition to Donald Trump's Immigration Executive Order

This executive order is one we do not support. . . . We're a nation of immigrants whose diverse backgrounds, ideas, and points of view have helped us build and invent as a nation for over 240 years.

—internal email, January 30, 2017

· ·

Keep Talented People in the United States

We do something which from a policy point of view in this country is clearly, in my opinion, malpractice, which is that we recruit the most talented students to come to our universities, and then, as soon as they graduate, we say, "No, you may not stay here." A lot of them would like to stay here, and these are people who would create jobs.

—*Charlie Rose*, November 16, 2012

· ·

The Growth of Amazon

Our growth has happened fast. Twenty years ago, I was driving boxes to the post office in my Chevy Blazer and dreaming of a forklift. In absolute numbers (as opposed to percentages), the past few years have been especially significant. We've grown from 30,000 employees in 2010 to more than 230,000 now. We're a bit like parents who look around one day and realize their kids are grown—you blink and it happens.

—letter to shareholders, April 6, 2016

ENTREPRENEURSHIP

••

Defining Entrepreneurship

Entrepreneurship is really more about a state of mind than it is about working for yourself. It's about being resourceful, it's about problem solving. If you meet people who seem like really good problem solvers, step back, and you'll see that they are self-reliant.

—Inc., April 1, 2004

••

Overnight Successes

I've noticed all overnight successes take about 10 years.

—Internet Association charity gala, May 2, 2017

••

A Beginner's Mind

That ability to look at things with a fresh mind, a beginner's mind, is very useful for entrepreneurs.

—Foreign Affairs, January/February 2015

Easy Ideas, Hard Results

It's easy to have ideas. It's very hard to turn an idea into a successful product. There are many steps in between, and it takes persistence.

—Edison Nation video series, April 2011

The Initial Business Plan

Writing the business plan, the initial hiring, getting the company incorporated. In a way they're sort of, you know, simple, almost pedestrian tasks. But that's how you start, one step at a time.

—American Academy of Achievement interview,
May 4, 2001

Be Realistic with Your Business

You can't sit down to write a business plan and say you're going to build a multibillion-dollar corporation; that's unrealistic. A good entrepreneur has a business idea that they believe they can make work at a much more reasonable scale and then proceeds adaptively from there, depending on what happens.

—*Foreign Affairs*, January/February 2015

It's very important for entrepreneurs to be realistic. And so if you believe on that first day, while you're writing the business plan, that there's a 70 percent chance that the whole thing will fail, then that kind of relieves the pressure of self-doubt. I mean, it's sort of like, I don't have any doubt about whether we're going to fail. That's the likely outcome. And it just is. And to pretend that it's not will lead you to do strange and, you know, unnatural things.

—American Academy of Achievement interview,
May 4, 2001

• •

Maintaining Optimism

My wife says, "If Jeff is unhappy, wait three minutes." I believe that optimism is an essential quality for doing anything hard—entrepreneurial endeavors or anything else. That doesn't mean that you're blind or unrealistic, it means that you keep focused on eliminating your risks, modifying your strategy, until it is a strategy about which you can be *genuinely* optimistic.

—*Inc.*, April 1, 2004

What to Do with Early Investments

What you do with those early, precious capital resources, is you go about systematically trying to eliminate risk.

—American Academy of Achievement interview,
May 4, 2001

Be Stubborn and Flexible

The trick to being an entrepreneur is to know when to be stubborn and when to be flexible. And my rule of thumb on that is to be stubborn on the big things and very flexible on the details.

—Wired's Disruptive by Design, June 15, 2009

Professional Swashbuckling

Without professionalism, swashbuckling just gets you killed.

—Vanity Fair New Establishment Summit,
October 20, 2016

How? What? Who?

When you start out, it's a one-person thing, at least on the first day, and you're not only figuring out what to do but actually doing it. At a certain point the company gets bigger, and you get to where you're mostly figuring out what to do but not how it's done. Eventually you get to the point where you're mostly figuring out who is going to do it, not even what to do. So one way to think about this is as a transition of questions, from "How?" to "What?" to "Who?"

—*Harvard Business Review*, October 2007

Laser Focus

Start-up companies need to be absolutely laser-focused, you know. So many start-up companies I see—and I talk to entrepreneurs and I see them—they have too many things going at once. And it's really, really important when you have these initial precious resources, and they're so very finite, that you need to be very focused.

—92nd Street Y in New York City, April 11, 2001

....

Start-Ups Need Luck

I believe that all start-up companies require huge amounts of luck.

—*Charlie Rose*, June 28, 2000

There are a lot of entrepreneurs. There are a lot of people who are very smart, very hardworking. Very few ever have, you know, the planetary alignment that leads to a tiny little company growing into something substantial. So that requires not only a lot of planning, a lot of hard work, a big team of people who are all dedicated, but it also requires that not only the planets align, but that, you know, you get a few galaxies in there aligning, too.

—American Academy of Achievement interview, May 4, 2001

The Danger of Managers

One of the differences between, sort of, founder/entrepreneurs and professional managers is that, you know, founder/entrepreneurs are stubborn about the vision and keep working on the details. And, you know, I think one of the dangers of bringing in professional managers to companies at times is that, if something's not working, the first thing they do is change the vision, and usually that's not the right thing to do.

—Wired's Disruptive by Design, June 15, 2009

Vision Triage

Once you have the big vision, you'll see that within it there are hundreds of smaller ones, and you need the ability to do brutal triage, to be able to say, "No, we don't do this, that, and that; we're going to focus exclusively on these three things."

—*Success*, July 1998

BUSINESS PRINCIPLES

....

Know the Obvious

Maintain a firm grasp of the obvious at all times.

—*Wired*, November 13, 2011

....

Looking for Answers

If you only do things where you know the answer in advance, your company goes away.

—*Esquire*, September 25, 2008

....

Humble and Paranoid

It pays to be humble and paranoid.

—A.B. Dick Lecture on Entrepreneurship, March 21, 1998

....

Stick to the Strategy

At the end of the day, you don't change your strategy because certain audiences don't understand it.

—Wired's Disruptive by Design, June 15, 2009

....

Be a Missionary

I strongly believe that missionaries make better products. They care more. For a missionary, it's not just about the business. There has to be a business, and the business has to make sense, but that's not why you do it. You do it because you have something meaningful that motivates you.

—*Fortune*, June 29, 2010

Mercenaries are trying to make a profit. Missionaries are trying to build the very best customer experience that they can. And, you know, the paradox of this is the missionaries usually end up making more money anyway.

—*The Kindle Chronicles*, July 26, 2016

....

More Than Shiny

A company shouldn't get addicted to being shiny, because shiny doesn't last. You really want something that's much deeper-keeled. You want your customers to value your service.

—*Wired*, November 13, 2011

....

One Industry, Many Companies

It's very rare for significant, meaningful industries to be built by single companies.

—Startup School, April 19, 2008

Base Your Strategy on the Things That Won't Change

The most important things are not the kind of big transitions. The most important things are the big pieces of stability, the rocks in the future that you can count on because you know they'll be there.

—*ABC News*, September 25, 2013

I very rarely get asked "What's *not* going to change in the next five to ten years?" At Amazon we're always trying to figure that out, because you can really spin up flywheels around those things. All the energy you invest in them today will still be paying you dividends ten years from now.

—*Harvard Business Review*, October 2007

The mistake that companies make is that when the external world changes suddenly, they can lose confidence and chase the newest wave.

—*New York Times*, May 19, 2002

If you base your strategy first and foremost on more transitory things—who your competitors are, what kind of technologies are available, and so on—those things are going to change so rapidly that you're going to have to change your strategy very rapidly, too.

—*Harvard Business Review*, October 2007

∙∙∙

Complaining Isn't a Strategy

One of the first rules of business is that complaining is not a strategy. And so, you know, you have to work with the world as you find it, not as you would have it be.

—The Future of Newspapers, June 21, 2017

∙∙∙

The Motivation of Customer Service

One of the good things about taking a customer-centric approach instead of a competitor-centric approach is that if you get ahead in a particular field or particular arena, then you end up still being very motivated. Whereas if you're very competitor-focused, it's really difficult to stay motivated when you're number one in a particular arena.

—Liberty Science Center Genius Gala 4.0,
May 1, 2015

Don't Discuss the Competition

We have a long history, that I like, of not talking about other companies.

—Startup School, April 19, 2008

Dealing with Competition

One way to not become complacent is to always have the beginner's mind. Have the mindset that you are the naïve one at this poker game, and there's probably somebody out there, unknown to you, who is doing a better job for the customer than you are.

—ShopSmart Shopping Summit, May 11, 2011

All we need to do is find *a* dimension where *a* competitor is better than us and we can celebrate that. Because then we know it's an existence proof. If they can do it, we can do it. So then we go and we try to do it as well as them.

—ShopSmart Shopping Summit, May 11, 2011

Developing New Skills

It's important to take an inventory of your skills, know what you're good at, and then, you know, try to do things that match up with your skills. But if you only do that, in our view, then eventually you will be outmoded, because your customers will eventually need things that you don't have skills for.

—D: All Things Digital, May 27, 2008

Word of Mouth

If you're not doing something that people will remark on, then it's going to be hard to generate word of mouth.

—*Bloomberg Businessweek*, August 1, 2004

Investors versus Managers

There is a good division of labor in the world, and management teams . . . have a very hard job, which is to try and build an important and lasting company. Wall Street analysts and investors have a different very hard job, which is to try and figure out how much that company is worth.

—*Charlie Rose*, April 2, 1999

Short-Term and Long-Term Investors

If you're going to invest in an internet stock—it's really true of technology stocks in general, but internet stocks in particular—you must be a long-term investor. And if you're a small investor, it should be a small portion of your portfolio, just because of the volatility.

—*Bloomberg*, July 14, 2002

It's very difficult to please short-term investors. I think it's a mistake, because to please short-term investors, you have to make trade-offs which are not in the interest of your customers. Whereas what long-term investors want to do, they want you to figure out how to please your customers.

—92nd Street Y in New York City, April 11, 2001

How to Know Share Value

If you could know for certain just two things—a company's future cash flows and its future number of shares outstanding—you would have an excellent idea of the fair value of a share of that company's stock today.

—letter to shareholders, April 18, 2002

Don't Focus on Short-Term Profitability

Do we have to be a profitable company? Yes! No company gets to keep doing anything unless they're profitable. If you want to be a sustaining and durable franchise, you have to do that. But we believe it would be the most shortsighted, horrible decision a management team could make to focus today on maximizing short-term profitability.

—*Dallas Morning News*, August 1999

We were profitable in December of 1995, six months after opening. And that was the worst mistake any company could have made, because when you are growing week over week at such high growth rates, and clearly have a value proposition that customers love, you need to be figuring out how to invest in that.

—*Charlie Rose*, June 28, 2000

••

Inputs over Outputs

Senior leaders that are new to Amazon are often surprised by how little time we spend discussing actual financial results or debating projected financial outputs. To be clear, we take these financial outputs seriously, but we believe that focusing our energy on the controllable inputs to our business is the most effective way to maximize financial outputs over time.

—letter to shareholders, April 14, 2010

••

Focus on Growth, Then Efficiency

What you should be doing is instead of investing all of that executive bandwidth, time, energy, [and] hardworking people on trying to get that 1 percent operating efficiency, you should instead be trying to build a company of the scale where 1 percent matters.

—92nd Street Y in New York City, April 11, 2001

Invest Profits in the Company

We have a number of different businesses. Some of those businesses are more mature, they're highly profitable, they generate a lot of profit for the company. And then we can take those profits and invest in the bold bets, the newer ideas, the things that may or may not work, and then also, invest them in the things that are working really well, that are working so well that we want to double down on them.

—Federation of Indian Chambers of Commerce
and Industry, October 1, 2014

Sticking to the Knitting

The question is always, why not stick to the knitting? My point of view on sticking to the knitting is that it's not the right thing for most businesses to be that focused. It's true that you hone skills in a business. You learn to be really good at a few things, and you do want to extend out from those skills. But your customer needs change slowly over time.

—Utah Technology Council Hall of Fame,
November 30, 2012

Business Extensions

We do make decisions about business extensions in a very deliberate way. And we basically go in two directions. We work backwards from customer needs—that's very important—and we work forward from our skills.

—*Wired's Disruptive by Design*, June 15, 2009

How to Get Synergies

I'm a big believer in getting synergies through business contracts. If you are trying to get synergies through a merger, it so often doesn't work. That should be your approach of last resort.

—*Bloomberg*, July 14, 2002

Growing a Seed

When we plant a seed, it tends to take five to seven years before it has a meaningful impact on the economics of the company.

—*Harvard Business Review*, October 2007

••

Don't Follow the Stock Market

I do not follow the stock on a daily basis, and I don't think there's any information in it.

—Harvard Business Review, January 3, 2013

If the stock is up 10 percent this month, don't feel 10 percent smarter, because when the stock is down 10 percent some month you're going to have to feel 10 percent dumber, and it's not going to feel as good.

—Ignition, December 2, 2014

••

Don't Believe PR

When the PR is good, don't believe it; and when it's the opposite way, don't believe that either.

—Foreign Affairs, January/February 2015

••

Making Long-Term Plans

Say you want to solve world hunger. If you think in terms of a five-year time frame, you get really depressed; it's an intractable problem. But if you say, well, let's see how we could solve this in 100 years—it's a problem because you'll be dead by then, but the solution becomes more tractable.

—Time, December 27, 1999

••

Don't Shrink

You can't shrink your way into relevance.

—The Future of Newspapers, June 21, 2017

••

Earning Your Reputation

Reputation is a trailing indicator of excellence.

—Amazon press conference, June 18, 2014

That's how you earn trust. Make a hard promise. Keep it. And if we can continue to earn trust, that's also what lets us branch out into new product categories, new businesses, because customers will give you the benefit of the doubt.

—*Charlie Rose*, July 28, 2010

Brands for companies are like reputations for people. And reputations are hard-earned and easily lost.

—Edison Nation video series, April 2011

You can't just decide, you know, you're going to have a new identity one day and a new reputation. You really need to look at the truth of the past and the history and uncover something that already exists—and then double down on that and make that your reputation.

—The Future of Newspapers, June 21, 2017

••

Reputation Is Worth More Than Money

You could say we will disappoint some small fraction of people but we will make a lot more money. But if you disappoint people, you lose brand reputation, and that's worth a lot more to us right now than money.

—*New York Times*, November 28, 1999

••

Don't Pretend to Be Something You're Not

What you absolutely cannot do—but you do see businesses try this—is they pretend to be something they're not. Even when people do advertise, the ones who advertise effectively are those who figure out what real value they genuinely bring, and then they shout about that.

—*Bloomberg Businessweek*, August 1, 2004

••

Tight Lips

There's no reason in business, usually, to boast about your accomplishments.

—*Charlie Rose*, October 27, 2016

An Abstract Brand

You can have a brand name which stands for a particular product category, but in my opinion, that brand will not be as valuable and robust as a brand which stands for something more abstract.

—*Charlie Rose*, June 27, 2001

Establishing Processes

Good process serves you so you can serve customers. But if you're not watchful, the process can become the thing. This can happen very easily in large organizations. The process becomes the proxy for the result you want. You stop looking at outcomes and just make sure you're doing the process right. Gulp.

—letter to shareholders, April 12, 2017

When you are inexperienced with disciplined process management, you initially think that it's equivalent to bureaucracy. But effective process is not bureaucracy. Bureaucracy is senseless processing—and we've had some of that, too.

—*Harvard Business Review*, October 2007

Fact-Based and Judgment-Based Decisions

The great thing about fact-based decisions is that they overrule the hierarchy. The most junior person in the company can win an argument with the most senior person with a fact-based decision.

—*Fast Company*, August 1, 2004

Math-based decisions command wide agreement, whereas judgment-based decisions are rightly debated and often controversial, at least until put into practice and demonstrated. Any institution unwilling to endure controversy must limit itself to decisions of the first type. In our view, doing so would not only limit controversy—it would also significantly limit innovation and long-term value creation.

—letter to shareholders, April 21, 2006

Disagree and Commit

Use the phrase "disagree and commit." This phrase will save a lot of time. If you have conviction on a particular direction even though there's no consensus, it's helpful to say, "Look, I know we disagree on this but will you gamble with me on it? Disagree and commit?" By the time you're at this point, no one can know the answer for sure, and you'll probably get a quick yes.

—letter to shareholders, April 12, 2017

Making Fast Decisions

Most decisions should probably be made with somewhere around 70% of the information you wish you had. If you wait for 90%, in most cases, you're probably being slow.

—letter to shareholders, April 12, 2017

"You've worn me down" is an awful decision-making process. It's slow and de-energizing. Go for quick escalation instead—it's better.

—letter to shareholders, April 12, 2017

Let's be fast. Let's try things quickly. Let's be decisive. We don't need to make these decisions by consensus. Most of these things are going to be two-way doors. If we try something that's wrong, doesn't work, we'll just back up and come back through the door again.

—The Future of Newspapers, June 21, 2017

CUSTOMER SERVICE

•••

Customer Obsession

The core of the company is customer obsession as opposed to competitor obsession.

—Vanity Fair New Establishment Summit,
October 20, 2016

•••

Missionaries for Customer Service

What I felt from the beginning was that it's important to have a mission that's bigger than ourselves, the way Sony did after the Second World War. They wanted to make Japan synonymous with quality, rather than cheap copies. And they succeeded brilliantly. Our mission is to create a new level of expectation in customers, which will cause all companies to raise their level. And if we can do that, that would be truly meaningful. That'll be something we can tell our grandchildren about. That's the difference between a mission and a job. If it's a job, then you won't have stories to tell your grandchildren.

—*Guardian*, February 10, 2001

Other organizations, whether they be other companies or whether they be hospitals or government agencies, whatever the organization is, they should look at Amazon as a role model and say, "How can we be as customer-centric as Amazon?"

—*Four Peaks*, September 13, 2013

• •

Knowing Your Customer

A remarkable customer experience starts with heart, intuition, curiosity, play, guts, taste. You won't find any of it in a survey.

—letter to shareholders, April 12, 2017

• •

Customer Service Defined

We have a very precise definition for customer-centric. It means listen, invent, and personalize.

—*Charlie Rose*, June 28, 2000

• •

Listen

Listen to customers, but don't *just* listen to customers—also invent on their behalf.

—letter to shareholders, April 14, 2010

Invent

We don't want to start with an idea and work toward the customer. We want to start with a customer problem and then invent to a solution.

—*Bloomberg Businessweek*, August 1, 2004

You have to remember that it's not the customer's job to invent for themselves. You know, every one of our customers has their own job, and they're inventing for their customers. And if you do focus groups and things, you will oftentimes be led astray when it comes to invention, because customers don't necessarily know in specific ways what it is that they would want.

—92nd Street Y in New York City, April 11, 2001

Personalize

People want better than average—they want exactly what's right for them.

—press release, December 22, 1998

We can use advanced technology—and we are, as I said, starting to do this now—to not only understand our products on a product-by-product individual basis, but to understand our customers on a customer-by-customer individualized basis.

—A.B. Dick Lecture on Entrepreneurship, March 21, 1998

•••

Reducing Friction

We live in a complex world, and if you can figure out how to make things simpler for people, they will value that.

—*Charlie Rose*, February 26, 2009

When you lower friction, you always get more of whatever behavior you made easier.

—Wired's Disruptive by Design, June 15, 2009

•••

Building Great Service for One Customer

We're not trying to build a great service for tens of millions of customers. We're trying to build a great service for one customer. If you think about it that way, the consequence of building a great service for one customer is you can get millions.

—Amazon press conference, June 18, 2014

Customer Service from the CEO Down

When it comes to the way we relentlessly drive down our consumer-facing pricing, I still continually launder and inspect that and talk to the people who do the work all the way through that whole chain. I need to be sure that we are in fact competitive and focused on offering our customers the lowest possible prices. That's one of the things I think is so highly leveraged that I am involved from heading level one all the way to heading level five.

—*Harvard Business Review*, October 2007

The Most Permanent Business Strategy

If you base your business strategy on things that are going to change, then you have to constantly change your strategy. Whereas if you formulate your strategy around customer needs, those tend to be stable in time.

—*Charlie Rose*, February 26, 2009

••

Customers and Shareholders Align

I think long-term thinking squares the circle. Proactively delighting customers earns trust, which earns more business from those customers, even in new business arenas. Take a long-term view, and the interests of customers and shareholders align.

—letter to shareholders, April 12, 2013

••

Don't Rely on Customer Loyalty

The companies that rely on brand loyalty are insane. Customers will be loyal to you because you don't take them up on it. It is one of those paradoxes. There is no resting on your laurels.

—*Playboy*, February 2000

I constantly remind our employees to be afraid, to wake up every morning terrified. Not of our competition, but of our customers. Our customers have made our business what it is, they are the ones with whom we have a relationship, and they are the ones to whom we owe a great obligation. And we consider them to be loyal to us—right up until the second that someone else offers them a better service.

—letter to shareholders, March 5, 1999

Earning Trust with Customers

How do you earn trust? Well, I can tell you how you
don't do it. You don't ask for it. That never works.
I think there is a simple recipe for earning trust.
It's hard to execute, hard to do, but it's simple to
describe. Here's how you earn trust. Step one: do
hard things well. Step two: repeat.

—Amazon press conference, June 18, 2014

Negative Reviews

Our point of view is, no, we make money when we
help customers make purchase decisions. Negative
reviews are helpful in making purchase decisions.
So it's a very customer-centric point of view. Negative reviews will be helpful for customers, and that
will ultimately sell more products than if you tried
to cherry-pick the reviews.

—*Bloomberg Businessweek*, August 1, 2004

••

Convince Customers Not to Spend Their Money

Some of my proudest moments are when customers tell me that we talked them out of buying something. It's a huge service for customers. With most
things, the amount you pay for the product isn't the
biggest cost; it is the time you spend with the product afterward.

—*Playboy*, February 2000

••

More Work, Less Talk

Our decision to put dollars into lower prices and
free shipping instead of TV advertising continues
to be embraced by customers.

—press release, October 21, 2004

You want to spend 70 percent of your time building
great customer experience and 30 percent of your
time shouting about it.

—*Charlie Rose*, April 2, 1999

Keep Customers Informed

The world is getting increasingly transparent—that information perfection is on the rise. If you believe that, it becomes strategically smart to align yourself with the customer.

—*Harvard Business Review*, October 2007

If you have a business model that in part relies upon your customers being misinformed—or, let's just say, incompletely informed—you'd better start working on changing your business model.

—AWS re: Invent, November 29, 2012

A Polarizing Company

From a customer point of view, we're not a very polarizing company. Pretty much everybody, even our harshest critics, will agree that we do a good job for customers. So we're sort of, unfortunately, dull in that way, which I consider to be really important. And then, when it comes to the stock, it's an incredibly polarizing story. You know, we have people who are fantastic fans who have been with us all along, and then we have people who just think that this is, you know, the worst possible investment that anybody could make.

—92nd Street Y in New York City, April 11, 2001

....

Keeping the Customer Present

If you really are customer-centric it's like being the host of a party. You're holding the party for your guests. Sometimes the host of the party is holding the party for the host of the party.

—*The Lead with Jake Tapper*, September 25, 2013

In almost any company, in fact, if you have a meeting, no matter how important the meeting is, there's always one important party who's not represented at the meeting, and it's the customer. So it's very easy inside a company to forget about the customer. Hopefully if you were to walk around Amazon.com and ask people, you know, why do you do something this way, a lot of the time, I hope, you'd hear the answer, "Because it's better for the customer."

—*Charlie Rose*, May 26, 1999

....

Solutions Come from the Customer

There's an old Warren Buffett story, that he has three boxes on his desk: in-box, out-box, and too hard. Whenever we're facing one of those too-hard problems, where we get into an infinite loop and can't decide what to do, we try to convert it into a straightforward problem by saying, "Well, what's better for the consumer?"

—*Harvard Business Review*, October 2007

•••

Customer Communities

The neat thing about customer reviews is that it's customers helping customers make purchase decisions. And that's what community is. Community is neighbors helping neighbors. You know you live in a community if you can knock on your neighbor's door, get a cup of sugar. Businesses cannot create community. All businesses can do is facilitate community.

—Association of American Publishers,
March 18, 1999

•••

Automated Customer Service

We build automated systems that look for occasions when we've provided a customer experience that isn't up to our standards, and those systems then proactively refund customers.

—letter to shareholders, April 12, 2013

Customer Service Creates Efficiencies

Any customer service agent can pull a product off of the Amazon website if they think that there's a problem. And then of course that sets in—having pulled that product off—that sets in place a whole series of processes that go back that we're not going to ship the same table to the same customer over and over.

—AWS re: Invent, November 29, 2012

Eliminate Defects, Eliminate Contacts

That's the best customer service. Find the defects that drove the contact. Work those defects all the way back to their true root cause.

—ShopSmart Shopping Summit, May 11, 2011

Our version of a perfect customer experience is one in which our customer doesn't want to talk to us. Every time a customer contacts us, we see it as a defect.

—*Wired*, November 13, 2011

The only contacts should be people saying, "I just had this thought I should thank you guys."

—ShopSmart Shopping Summit, May 11, 2011

CORPORATE CULTURE

....

Building a Team

This is probably the biggest single component . . . bringing together a talented and diverse group of people. That is absolutely key. You attract them by giving them the opportunity to build something important, to improve customers' lives, and to change the world in some fundamental way. Great people should also be owners, and they are, through our generous stock-option incentives.

—*Success*, July 1998

A single individual cannot keep in touch with the plethora of, you know, of new things happening. So what you have to do is, you have to put in place a recruiting process that attracts and retains smart, talented, hardworking people who want to be a part of your mission.

—*Charlie Rose*, June 28, 2000

Any important achievement that you can think of and pursue in life, it's going to turn out to be teamwork.

—opening of Apollo exhibit at the Museum of Flight, May 20, 2017

• •

Self-Reinforcing Culture

People here like to invent, and as a result other people who like to invent are attracted here. And people who don't like to invent are uncomfortable here. So it's self-reinforcing.

—*Fortune*, May 26, 2003

• •

Hire Inventors

When I interview people I ask them to give me an example of something they've invented. And I always point out it doesn't have to be something that you actually took to the patent office, but it could be a metric that you invented and followed carefully, it could be a business process that you invented. You want to select people who like to invent their way out of boxes.

—Utah Technology Council Hall of Fame,
November 30, 2012

••

Invention at Every Level

You need to hire people who like to build, who like to invent—and you need to make sure that they like to do that at all granularities. You know, sometimes you come across these people who are only interested in inventing at the grandest sort of whiteboard level, and they actually can't make progress in the real world.

—Conference on Entrepreneurship at Stanford
University, February 12, 2005

••

Hire People You Admire

If you think about the people you've admired in your life, they are probably people you've been able to learn from or take an example from. For myself, I've always tried hard to work only with people I admire, and I encourage folks here to be just as demanding. Life is definitely too short to do otherwise.

—letter to shareholders, March 5, 1999

••

Work Long, Hard, and Smart

It's not easy to work here (when I interview people I tell them, "You can work long, hard, or smart, but at Amazon.com you can't choose two out of three"), but we are working to build something important, something that matters to our customers, something that we can all tell our grandchildren about. Such things aren't meant to be easy.

—letter to shareholders, March 30, 1998

••

An Employee Should Want to Work Here

An employee staying somewhere they don't want to be isn't healthy for the employee or the company.

—letter to shareholders, April 10, 2014

••

An Informal Atmosphere

We have an informal atmosphere, which I think helps people tell me no—and not just me. It's also really important that they be able to say what they think to their senior vice president or vice president and so on. An informal atmosphere, I think, is a huge benefit.

—*Harvard Business Review*, October 2007

Be Serious, Have Fun

There is no contradiction between being intense and having fun. You can absolutely do that. That's what we try to achieve, and at our best it is what we achieve. We'll have some big problems, we'll get together, and we'll laugh about them.

—*Harvard Business Review*, October 2007

Response to *New York Times* Article Criticizing Amazon's Workplace

[The *New York Times* article] claims that our intentional approach is to create a soulless, dystopian workplace where no fun is had and no laughter heard. Again, I don't recognize this Amazon and I very much hope you don't, either. More broadly, I don't think any company adopting the approach portrayed could survive, much less thrive, in today's highly competitive tech hiring market.

—internal memo, August 2015

His Leadership Role

I can do some things at Amazon that would be hard for other people to do only because of my history with the company.

—Ignition, December 2, 2014

Maintaining the Culture

My main job today: I work hard at helping to maintain the culture. A culture of high standards of operational excellence, of inventiveness, of willingness to fail, willingness to make bold experiments. I'm the counterbalance to the institutional "no" who can say "yes."

—*Business Insider*, December 13, 2014

You can write down your corporate culture, but when you do so, you're discovering it, uncovering it—not creating it. It is created slowly over time by the people and by events—by the stories of past success and failure that become a deep part of the company lore.

—letter to shareholders, April 6, 2016

What Senior Leaders Do

The main job of a senior leader is to identify two or three important ideas and then to enforce great execution against those big ideas.

—Internet Association charity gala, May 2, 2017

• •

Senior Leaders in the Trenches

I've never met what I think of as a good executive who does not choose certain highly leveraged activities—some area they consider so important that they will inspect it all the way down to the how stage.

—*Harvard Business Review*, October 2007

I've not seen an effective manager or leader who can't spend some fraction of time down in the trenches. If they don't do that, they get out of touch with reality, and their whole thought and management process becomes abstract and disconnected.

—*Fortune*, May 26, 2003

• •

Advantages of an Urban Campus

Fifteen percent of our employees at headquarters live in the same zip code where they work. Twenty percent of our employees walk to work. So an urban campus is so much greener than a suburban campus . . . and it's also just way more vibrant, which I personally believe also helps Amazon because it keeps people connected with this vibrant urban area.

—Ignition, December 2, 2014

••

Two-Pizza Rule

No team should be so large that it cannot be fed with just two pizzas. And so obviously to do great things you need big teams, but you need to subdivide them. . . . If you can arrange to do big things with a multitude of small teams—and that takes a lot of effort to organize that way—but if you can figure that out, the communication on those small teams will be very natural and easy.

—Pathfinder Awards, October 22, 2016

••

The Six-Page Memo

All of our meetings are structured around a six-page narrative memo, and when you have to write your ideas out in complete sentences and complete paragraphs, it forces a deeper clarity of thinking.

—*Charlie Rose*, November 16, 2012

How to Do Meetings

Most meetings should be used for a kind of mild brainstorming or something like that, where you're really doing a lot of wandering. Wandering is super important. Thinking you know exactly where you're going is a kind of lack of humility that doesn't let you invent.

—Code Conference, June 1, 2016

Around a Whiteboard

If I could organize my day just in terms of pure enjoyment, I would just be with other people around a whiteboard.

—*Charlie Rose*, November 16, 2012

Maintain Humility

While it may seem to people on the outside that Amazon.com is on top of the world, and it's a perfectly reasonable thing to wonder, internally we try very hard not to think that way.

—*Dallas Morning News*, August 1999

··

Jeff Bezos's Desk

[Bezos's desk, which was made of a door and four 2 × 4's] is a symbol of spending money on things that matter to customers and not spending money on things that don't.

—*60 Minutes Overtime*, February 3, 1999

··

Low Salaries

We pay very low cash compensation relative to most companies. We also have no incentive compensation of any kind. And the reason we don't is because it is detrimental to teamwork.

—*Fortune*, November 16, 2012

··

Paid Volunteers

Paid volunteers are the best people to work with as they're here for the right reasons.

—*Telegraph*, August 16, 2015

INVENTION AND INNOVATION

••

Evolved to Explore

I think it's probably a survival skill that we're curious and like to explore. Our ancestors, who were incurious and failed to explore, probably didn't live as long as the ones who were looking over the next mountain range to see if there were more sources of food and better climates and so on and so on.

—*Business Insider*, December 13, 2014

••

Lean Toward the Future

If you're leaning away from the future, the future's going to win every time.

—Vanity Fair New Establishment Summit,
October 20, 2016

••

Looking Ahead to Innovation

I do think there's more innovation ahead of us than there is behind us.

—TED Talk, February 2003

. . . .

Dreamers and Builders

Dreamers come first. The dreamers dream. . . . Then builders come along, and with that inspiration, some of this stuff comes true.

—*Charlie Rose*, November 16, 2012

. . . .

Following *Star Trek*

We as humanity, as a civilization, as a technological civilization, are still quite a ways away from being able to be as magical and amazing as the *Star Trek* computer. We still have a couple of centuries. I don't think we'll need that much time, actually.

—The Washington Post's Transformers, May 18, 2016

. . . .

Day One and Day Two

Day Two is stasis. Followed by irrelevance. Followed by excruciating, painful decline. Followed by death. And that is why it is always Day One.

—Amazon All-Hands, March 2017

I think it's Day Two when the rate of change slows. And so far the rate of change on the internet, if anything, is accelerating.

—*Charlie Rose*, November 16, 2012

An Explorer Mentality

Some companies, if you wanted to put it into a single word, they have a conqueror mentality, and we have an explorer mentality.

—*Harvard Business Review*, January 3, 2013

People Need to Build

Morale comes not from things that you layer on to make people happy. It comes from being able to build. People like to build. The question is, Could it be done? The answer is, Absolutely.

—*Esquire*, January 29, 2007

Taking Weird Paths

Invention always leads you down paths that people are going to think are weird.

—Conference on Entrepreneurship at Stanford University, February 12, 2005

Two Kinds of Critics

Any time you do anything new, there will be critics. There will be two kinds of critics: sincere critics and people who have a vested interest in the old way, who have . . . a financial interest to be critics.

—ShopSmart Shopping Summit, May 11, 2011

••

Responding to Criticism

When you receive criticism from well-meaning people, it pays to, first of all, search yourself. Are they right? And if they are, you need to adapt what you're doing. If they're not right, if you really have conviction that they're not right, then you need to have that long-term willingness to be misunderstood. It's a key part of invention.

—The Aspen Institute's 26th Annual Awards Dinner,
November 5, 2009

You go back in time, and we've been called Amazon .toast, Amazon.con, Amazon.bomb. This is all, like, in the first three years of our existence. And that's part of what I'm talking about—the willingness to be misunderstood.

—*Charlie Rose*, July 28, 2010

••

Accepting Change

It's very difficult for incumbents who have a sweet thing to accept change. It's just very difficult. It's very easy, but almost always incorrect, to glamorize the past.

—*Business Insider*, December 13, 2014

Stubborn and Flexible

The thing about inventing is you have to be both stubborn and flexible, more or less simultaneously. Of course, the hard part is figuring out when to be which!

—*Fast Company*, August 1, 2004

The Business of Invention

The thing I love is the inventing. So I do the business, and I enjoy it, but I don't love it. The thing that I love is getting with one of our product teams and figuring out things like, you know, the next generation of customer reviews.

—*Charlie Rose*, June 28, 2000

Why Not?

People in this business spend a lot of time looking at ideas and asking, why do that? But sometimes the more powerful question is, why not?

—*Wired*, April 21, 2008

Successful Experiments Enable New Ones

One of my jobs is to encourage people to be bold. It's incredibly hard. Experiments are, by their very nature, prone to failure. A few big successes compensate for dozens and dozens of things that didn't work. Bold bets—Amazon Web Services, Kindle, Amazon Prime, our third-party seller business—all of those things are examples of bold bets that did work, and they pay for a lot of experiments.

—*Business Insider*, December 13, 2014

Invention in a Large Company

We want to be a large company that's also an invention machine. We want to combine the extraordinary customer-serving capabilities that are enabled by size with the speed of movement, nimbleness, and risk-acceptance mentality normally associated with entrepreneurial start-ups.

—letter to shareholders, April 6, 2016

To do clean-sheet invention inside a larger company, you need a culture that high fives these tiny little fast-growing businesses. And that's pretty rare.

—Wired's Disruptive by Design, June 15, 2009

Success Has Many Fathers

There's a saying: failure is an orphan and success has many fathers. That's a very true saying, and it captures something very deep, that anything at large scale that gets done and is successful, you can count on the fact that there genuinely were many fathers.

—CNBC, September 25, 2013

Reduce the Costs of Experiments

The way to get a lot of innovation in a company, in my opinion . . . is to work very, very hard to reduce the cost of doing experiments. Because the problem is, if experiments are expensive, then very few people are going to get to do very few experiments.

—lecture to the MIT ACM/IEEE Club,
November 25, 2002

Big Things Start Small

Big things start small. You know, the biggest oak starts from an acorn. If you want to do anything new, you've got to be willing to let that acorn grow into a little sapling, and then finally into a small tree, and maybe one day it'll be a big business on its own.

—*Four Peaks*, September 13, 2013

Long-Term Goals Foster Innovation

If we needed to see meaningful financial results in two to three years, some of the most meaningful things we've done we would never have even started.

—*Harvard Business Review*, January 3, 2013

Don't Give Up Too Soon

I think most companies, especially larger companies, give up on things too soon.

—Code Conference, June 1, 2016

Courting Controversy

Amazon.com must continue to be an innovative pioneer, and pioneers inevitably create some controversy, as we did four years ago when we first let customers post negative reviews of books and as we did one year ago when we started publishing storewide sales rankings. The one thing that we'd like everyone to know is that even as we explore the unknown, we'll always be trying to do the right thing, and we'll always be listening to our customers.

—press release, August 26, 1999

Be Nimble and Robust

The thing for companies is you need to be nimble and robust. So you need to be able to take a punch, and you also need to be quick and innovative and doing new things at a high speed. That's the best defense against the future.

—Vanity Fair New Establishment Summit,
October 20, 2016

Going Beyond the Textbook

While many of our systems are based on the latest in computer science research, this often hasn't been sufficient: our architects and engineers have had to advance research in directions that no academic had yet taken. Many of the problems we face have no textbook solutions, and so we—happily—invent new approaches.

—letter to shareholders, April 28, 2011

Blind Alleys

We even like going down alleys that turn out to be blind alleys. Of course, every once in a while, one of those blind alleys opens up into a broad avenue. And that's really fun.

—Amazon press conference, September 6, 2012

∙∙

Capturing Attention

Attention is the scarce commodity of the late 20th century. And one of the ways that you can [capture attention], and it's the way that we did it, is by doing something new and innovative for the first time that actually has real value for the customer.

—Special Libraries Association conference, June 1997

∙∙

Me Too Strategies

If you're competitor-focused, you have to wait until there is a competitor doing something. Being customer-focused allows you to be more pioneering. We have found that, on the Internet, "me too" strategies seem not to work very well.

—*U.S. News & World Report*, November 19, 2008

If 100 companies are doing something, and you're the 101st, you're not really bringing any value to society.

—*Charlie Rose*, November 16, 2012

Close Following on the Internet

The rate of change in the online world is so rapid that close following doesn't work as well as it might in a more stable industry that changes more slowly over time.

—Conference on Entrepreneurship at Stanford University, February 12, 2005

Pioneers and Copycats

It appears to me just empirically that if you invent a new way of doing something, typically, if you're lucky, you get about two years of runway before competitors copy your idea.

—*Charlie Rose*, October 27, 2016

There's a strong case to be made for being a copier. It's just not as satisfying, or as fun!

—*Wired*, March 1, 1999

The Amazon Way

When we do things, we have to have some twist, there has to be some innovation, there has to be something where customers are saying, "Yeah, that's what I would expect from Amazon."

—*Charlie Rose*, June 27, 2001

··

Barnes & Noble

B&N isn't doing any innovation at all on the Web—all they do is copy Amazon feature for feature, sometimes down to the exact wording. Is that right?

—Oreilly.com, March 2, 2000

··

Don't Reinvent the Wheel

It's very important when you're doing something new not to reinvent the wheel on stuff where you're not actually creating any new value.

—Edison Nation video series, April 2011

··

Invent and Improve

True innovation is something that's not only an invention but an improvement. It's not hard to make things different, but it is hard to make things different and better.

—Edison Nation video series, April 2011

··

Invention and Disruption

We don't seek to disrupt, we seek to delight.

—*Telegraph*, August 16, 2015

Invention is not disruptive. Only customer adoption is disruptive. At Amazon, we've invented a lot of things that customers did not care about at all, and believe me, they were not disruptive to anyone.

—Internet Association charity gala, May 2, 2017

Reinventing Normal

Nothing gives us more pleasure at Amazon than *"reinventing normal"*—creating inventions that customers love and resetting their expectations for what normal should be.

—letter to shareholders, April 10, 2014

Forever Young

If your customer base is aging with you, then eventually you're going to become obsolete or irrelevant. And so you need to be constantly figuring out who are your new customers or what are you doing to stay forever young.

—*ABC News*, September 25, 2013

• •

Enabling Creativity

The most radical and transformative of inventions are often those that empower *others* to unleash *their* creativity—to pursue *their* dreams.

—letter to shareholders, April 13, 2012

Even well-meaning gatekeepers slow innovation. When a platform is self-service, even the improbable ideas can get tried, because there's no expert gatekeeper ready to say "that will never work!" And guess what—many of those improbable ideas do work, and society is the beneficiary of that diversity.

—letter to shareholders, April 13, 2012

• •

Do New Things Kill Old Things?

Every time a new technological innovation comes along, it predicts the demise of the old thing. When television came along, everyone predicted the demise of the movie theater, and they were wrong, of course. Movies got bigger and better than ever.

—*Dallas Morning News*, August 1999

• •

Education Drives the Economy

A long time ago, people thought it was raw materials that drove the economy. Whichever country had more gold was the richest country. That's not true anymore. What drives economies is the education of the people and the innovation that they can then create.

—*Charlie Rose*, June 27, 2001

• •

Don't Punish Failure

On the big things we cannot do as many experiments per unit time as we can on the small things, and so they have to be somewhat more carefully chosen. But even there, it would be an unreasonable bar to expect that they will all work, even the big ones.

—ShopSmart Shopping Summit, May 11, 2011

Choose Experiments Carefully
(But Don't Expect Them to Work)

The executives running those failures move on to bigger and greater things. They don't get, you know, sidelined or, you know, told to go away. If you want really good people to take on bold initiatives that might not work, they can't be worried. They can't be thinking, "Actually, I really only want to work on a sure thing."

—Federation of Indian Chambers of Commerce and Industry, October 1, 2014

Failure Is Key

I believe we are the best place in the world to fail (we have plenty of practice!), and failure and invention are inseparable twins. To invent you have to experiment, and if you know in advance it's going to work, it's not an experiment.

—letter to shareholders, April 6, 2016

Keeping the Vision

After every failure, we ask ourselves, "Do we still believe in the vision?" If we have conviction, that gives us energy to pursue [another] approach.

—*Fortune*, May 26, 2009

Cost of Failure

Very rarely is failure very expensive. The big costs that most companies incur are much harder to notice, and those are the errors of omission.

—Wired's Disruptive by Design, June 15, 2009

The Bad Kind of Failure

There's a different kind of failure which is not what you want. That's where you have operating history and you do know what you're doing and you just screw it up.

—Internet Association charity gala, May 2, 2017

Expertise in a Child's Mind

You have to have a certain childlike ability to not be trapped by your expertise. And that fresh look, that beginner's mind, once you're an expert, is unbelievably hard to maintain. But great inventors are always looking. They have a certain divine discontent. They may have seen something a thousand times and still, it occurs to them that that thing, even though they're accustomed to it, could be improved.

—Liberty Science Center Genius Gala 4.0,
May 1, 2015

Obstacles Are Opportunities

We like to look at obstacles as opportunities to invent instead of as problems.

—Federation of Indian Chambers of Commerce
and Industry, October 1, 2014

Both A and B

The right question is, how can we do A and B? What invention do we need to be able to do both?

—Utah Technology Council Hall of Fame,
November 30, 2012

Solving Problems

You say, "OK, now we're going to spend 15 minutes providing skepticism, picking this apart. And then we're going to force rank all of the reasons this won't work, and then we're going to find solutions to each of those." And so you can iterate through that.

—*Charlie Rose*, November 16, 2012

Improve Old Solutions

Most of the problems in the world already have solutions of one kind or another. All of those solutions can be improved upon. There's no chance that anything is perfected yet. I don't believe that.

—Edison Nation video series, April 2011

Working Back from the Solution

Sometimes people see the problem and the problem is really annoying them, and then they invent a solution. Sometimes you can work this from the backwards direction. And in fact in high tech I think a lot of the innovation sometimes comes from this direction. You see a new technology or there's something out there, some new understanding in the world, and you work backwards from a solution to find the appropriate problem.

—Conference on Entrepreneurship at Stanford
University, February 12, 2005

Freedom to Wander

Just because you're wandering doesn't mean you're lost, and that's a really important thing to keep in mind when you're trying to invent.

—Liberty Science Center Genius Gala 4.0,
May 1, 2015

· ·

Ideas Breed

The great thing about ideas is that every new idea leads to two more new ones. It's the opposite of a gold rush, where the more people who show up in 1849 to get that gold in California, the faster the gold runs out. Ideas are not like that; ideas breed.

—*Foreign Affairs*, January/February 2015

· ·

Update the Patent System

Patents are supposed to encourage innovation and we're starting to be in a world where they might start to stifle innovation. Governments may need to look at the patent system and see if those laws need to be modified because I don't think some of these battles are healthy for society.

—*Metro*, October 15, 2012

Think Long Term

We humans are getting so technologically capable that we need to think longer term. You know, 10,000 years ago we really couldn't do very much damage. And, you know, I think 100 years from now, 500 years from now, we're going to be able to do quite a bit of damage—and do great things. I'm super optimistic. I don't think we'll do that. I think we'll figure it all out.

—Pathfinder Awards, October 22, 2016

No Good Old Days

Everything about our society gets better over time. I really do believe that. I'm an optimist. You know, the myth of the "good old days" is usually just that—a myth.

—*Four Peaks*, September 13, 2013

TECHNOLOGY AND DEVICES

••

Technology Is in Everything

Technology infuses all of our teams, all of our processes, our decision-making, and our approach to innovation in each of our businesses. It is deeply integrated into everything we do.

—letter to shareholders, April 28, 2011

••

A Small AI Company

Amazon.com is very much a technology company. In fact, I think of us in many ways as sort of a small AI company.

—A.B. Dick Lecture on Entrepreneurship, March 21, 1998

Transformative Technology

In the physical world, retailers will continue to use technology to reduce costs, but not to transform the customer experience. We too will use technology to reduce costs, but the bigger effect will be using technology to drive adoption and revenue.

—letter to shareholders, April 13, 2001

Controlling Technology

We're trying to make it easier for people to stay in control of their technology instead of the technology being in control of the person.

—CNBC, September 25, 2013

Empower Other People's Creativity

Every time you figure out some way of providing tools and services that empower other people to deploy their creativity, you're really on to something.

—Vanity Fair New Establishment Summit,
October 20, 2016

When you have a new technology or a new medium, it can create a new art form, or sometimes reenliven old ones.

—*Charlie Rose*, November 19, 2007

••

Old Technologies

It's certainly the goal of any new technology to become an old technology.

—*Bloomberg*, July 14, 2002

••

Coevolution

We've coevolved with our tools for thousands of years. We change our tools, and our tools change us.

—Wired's Disruptive by Design, June 15, 2009

••

Cheap but Sophisticated

Work hard to charge less. Sell devices near break-even and you can pack a lot of sophisticated hardware into a very low price point.

—press release, October 25, 2012

We want to make money when people use our devices—not when people buy our devices. We think this aligns us better with customers. For example, we don't need our customers to be on the upgrade treadmill. We can be very happy to see people still using four-year-old Kindles!

—letter to shareholders, April 12, 2013

Gadgets versus Services

People don't want gadgets. They want services.

—*Charlie Rose*, November 16, 2012

Self-Important Devices

I hate self-important devices. . . . It's like the microwave oven that beeps at you until you open the door. . . . What you really want is for devices to get out of the way and leave you alone.

—The Aspen Institute's 26th Annual Awards Dinner, November 5, 2009

Multipurpose Devices

It's a myth that multipurpose devices are always better.

—Wired's Disruptive by Design, June 15, 2009

Customization

Customized things don't work as well.

—AWS re: Invent, November 29, 2012

•••

Entertainment Leads Technology

Entertainment in general, including tourism, often leads new technologies, and then those new technologies often circle back around and get used in very important utilitarian ways.

—The Washington Post's Transformers, May 18, 2016

•••

Amazon Web Services and the
Amazon Approach

AWS is a good example of how we approach ideas and risk-taking at Amazon. We strive to focus relentlessly on the customer, innovate rapidly, and drive operational excellence. We manage by two seemingly contradictory traits: impatience to deliver faster and a willingness to think long term.

—press release, April 23, 2015

How Amazon Web Services Started

We were really doing it initially for ourselves. As we were building this set of—they're called APIs, Application Programming Interfaces—as we were building this set of APIs, we realized if we did a little extra work we could externalize those APIs and sell them to others. And so we started a whole new business which focuses on a developer customer set, and that has been very successful. You know, I rarely run into a start-up company today that's not using Amazon Web Services' Elastic Compute Cloud.

—BookExpo America, May 30, 2008

The Purpose of Amazon Web Services

We want to find the useful guts of Amazon and expose them, expose them to the broader community and see if other people can find ways of using the guts of Amazon to surprise us.

—Web 2.0 podcast, October 5, 2004

The whole idea behind web services is to let companies focus on the parts of their business that are really important and differentiated about their business. And we don't want the services to be hard to learn.

—Startup School, April 19, 2008

● ●

Artificial versus Human Intelligence

We're still a long way away from being able to do things the way humans do things. Human-like intelligence is still pretty mysterious, even to the most advanced AI researchers. . . . If you think about how we learn, we're incredibly data-efficient. So when we train something like Alexa to recognize natural language, we use millions of data points, and we have to collect what's called a ground truth database. And it's a huge expensive effort to collect that ground truth database, and that becomes the training set that Alexa learns from. Humans learn incredibly data-efficiently. We only need a few examples.

—The Washington Post's Transformers, May 18, 2016

We still don't know how to build computers that think like human beings, but we're capable of solving problems that seemed unsolvable only 10 years ago. From medicine, to driverless cars, to language, it will be an enabling infrastructure and all the industries will use it.

—*La Repubblica*, July 24, 2016

••

Machine Learning

Rule-based systems can be used successfully, but they can be hard to maintain and can become brittle over time. In many cases, advanced machine learning techniques provide more accurate classification and can self-heal to adapt to changing conditions.

—letter to shareholders, April 28, 2011

••

AI Improves Everything

Machine learning and AI is a horizontal enabling layer. It will empower and improve every business, every government organization, every philanthropy. Basically, there's no institution in the world that cannot be improved with machine learning.

—Internet Association charity gala, May 2, 2017

••

AI in the US Government

The United States needs to, in every way, at every level, be working on machine learning and artificial intelligence, and that can be used in every part of government to improve the services that government provides to citizens.

—American Technology Council roundtable,
June 19, 2017

Specialized AI

I think there are going to be a bunch of artificially intelligent agents in the world. . . . I think you're going to find just, a bit like apps and websites, that there're going to be specialties, and you may not ask the same AI for everything.

—Code Conference, June 1, 2016

Alexa on the Enterprise

Our vision was that in the long term it would become the *Star Trek* computer. You could ask it anything and ask it to do things for you, ask it to find things for you, and then it would be easy to converse with in a very natural way.

—The Washington Post's Transformers, May 18, 2016

Voice Control

Experiences designed around the human voice will fundamentally improve the way people use technology.

—press release, June 25, 2015

Echo Everywhere

It's a communal device. Unlike a phone, which is a personal device. My kids—I have four kids—and my wife and I use it continuously. Everyone has their own playlists and music preferences and if they're all in the kitchen together they stomp on each other with their Alexa requests. It's cacophony with four kids in the house. And if you look at the recent [Consumer Electronics Show] announcements, you'll see most manufacturers are already laying in plans to put Echo and Alexa in the car.

—*Billboard*, February 9, 2017

Technology for Good and Bad

Technologies, in general, tend to be agnostic with respect to whether they could be used for good or used for evil. And I think that, you know, over the next 50 years, we are going to face a lot of very tough decisions as a society in how we make sure that we are harnessing those technologies for good purposes.

—American Academy of Achievement interview, May 4, 2001

Dangers of Biotechnology

I worry more about . . . weapons proliferation, including, you know, I think we're going to see extraordinary engineering advances in biotechnology. I think that that is going to come with a whole set of new ethical decisions. And not just ethical decisions about, like, do you want to, you know, make your children more beautiful, but very dangerous kinds of technologies that will be accessible to people who are not on the side of good.

—The Aspen Institute's 26th Annual Awards Dinner, November 5, 2009

Data Security

Data security is, it's one of these, you know, very dynamic situations where the bad guys get better and the good guys have to keep getting better too.

—ShopSmart Shopping Summit, May 11, 2011

New Laws for New Technologies

This is an issue of our age: privacy versus national security. This is a grand issue of our age, which means it needs to be looked at by the highest courts. It needs to be looked at by citizens and lawmakers.

—The Washington Post's Transformers, May 18, 2016

BOOKS AND KINDLE

··

Passionate about Books

Books are definitely a passion for me, too, though they are not the reason that Amazon.com started with books.

—Playboy, February 2000

··

Why Books?

I picked books because books are very unusual in one respect. And that is that there are more items in the book category than there are items in any other category, by far. There are millions of different books active and in print. I was also looking for something that you could only do on the Web. And having a bookstore with universal selection is only possible on the Web.

—Vanity Fair, July 2008

That was really the founding premise. If you go back and look at Amazon's original business plan, the way we were going to differentiate ourselves is by making it convenient and easy for people to find these hard-to-find books. And I think that that has made the whole ecosystem much more vibrant.

—BookExpo America, May 30, 2008

....

Making Life-Changing Books Accessible

Let's say right now there's a one-in-a-thousand chance that every time you walk into a bookstore you find one of these life-changing books. We want to make that a one-in-500 chance, work for another five years and make it a one-in-200 chance, and another five years and make it a one-in-100 chance.

—*Washington Post*, November 8, 1998

....

Bookstores Will Stay in Business Despite Amazon

Amazon.com is not going to put bookstores out of business. Barnes & Noble is opening a new superstore every four days. Borders is opening a new superstore every nine days.

—*Fast Company*, October 31, 1996

· ·

The Future of Bookselling

The internet is disrupting every media industry. . . . People can complain about that, but complaining is not a strategy. Amazon is not happening to bookselling. The future is happening to bookselling.

—*60 Minutes*, December 1, 2013

· ·

Sentimental about Bookstores

Sometimes I get asked about, you know, competitors, and do we worry about our competitors or do we feel bad for them in, you know, some cases. And sometimes we do. I can be very sentimental about bookstores and things like that. You know, I grew up as a kid reading physical books, and I can be as sentimental as the next person. But I also will say, you know, it's not our job to choose how people want to read.

—Utah Technology Council Hall of Fame, November 30, 2012

Books Are Too Expensive

If you want a healthy culture of reading book-length things, you've got to make books more accessible. . . . Part of that is making them less expensive. Books, in my view, are too expensive. You know, $30 for a book is too expensive. . . . If you just think . . . "I'm only competing against other $30 books," then you don't get there. But if you realize that you're really competing against, you know, Candy Crush . . . then you start to say, "Well, gosh, you know, maybe we should really work on reducing friction on long-form reading."

—Ignition, December 2, 2014

Selling Used Books on Amazon

When we first did it, people were very unhappy with us in the publishing industry, because, you know, we're putting these used books next to the new ones. And, you know, we're very simple-minded about things like that. If we think it's a good customer experience, our belief is, long term, it will be very good for the whole ecosystem. And I think that has proven out with used books. . . . A lot of people are much more willing to try an author if they can pay $4 to try the author. And, you know, the studies we've done have not demonstrated any cannibalization at all.

—BookExpo America, May 30, 2008

●●●

Kindle Announcement

We've been working on Kindle for more than three years. Our top design objective was for Kindle to disappear in your hands—to get out of the way—so you can enjoy your reading. We also wanted to go beyond the physical book. Kindle is wireless, so whether you're lying in bed or riding a train, you can think of a book, and have it in less than 60 seconds. No computer is needed—you do your shopping directly from the device.

—press release, November 19, 2007

●●●

You Can't Out-Book Books

We have to look for things that we can do with this technology that you could never do with a paper book, instead of trying to duplicate every last feature.

—*Charlie Rose*, November 19, 2007

••

Are E-books a Win for Publishers?

There are a lot of opportunities for all parties that will come out of e-books. So if you look at Kindle books from a publisher's point of view, they never go out of stock, you never print too many and then have to destroy the overprinting, and there's no cost, no physical cost, to do this.

—*IO Reporter*, February 6, 2011

••

E-book Efficiency

If you look at the efficiencies in the supply chain by not having to do all of that printing and all of the incremental unit sales that you will get from having the lower price point, authors are going to be read more, everybody's going to make more money, and the returns on invested capital are going to be higher because you're not going to have to have the heavy-duty, you know, CapEx expense that's associated with, you know, distribution, trucks, distribution printing facilities, and so on and so on.

—Wired's Disruptive by Design, June 15, 2009

••

Kindle Reading Rates

What we find is that when people buy a Kindle, they read four times as much as they did before they bought the Kindle.

—*BBC News*, October 11, 2012

••

Kindle Book Sales Overtake Print Book Sales

Customers are now choosing Kindle books more often than print books. We had high hopes that this would happen eventually, but we never imagined it would happen this quickly—we've been selling print books for 15 years and Kindle books for less than four years.

—press release, May 19, 2011

••

Unparalleled Profitability

Publishers are having unparalleled profitability, and the book industry is in better shape than it ever has been, and it's because of e-books.

—*Business Insider*, December 13, 2014

••

The Importance of Long-Form Narrative

What's really important is not the container, but it's the narrative. Long-form reading is important for our society.

—D: All Things Digital, May 27, 2008

I believe that we learn different things from long form than we learn from short form. Both are important. If you read *The Remains of the Day*, which is one of my favorite books, you can't help but come away and think, I just spent 10 hours living an alternate life and I learned something about life and about regret. You can't do that in a blog post.

—*Newsweek*, December 20, 2009

••

The Novel Won't Go Away

I think the novel will thrive in its current form. That doesn't mean that there won't be new narrative inventions as well. There very well may be. In fact, there probably will be. But I don't think they'll displace the novel.

—*Newsweek*, December 20, 2009

Quest for Attention

We hope Kindle and its successors may gradually and incrementally move us over years into a world with longer spans of attention, providing a counterbalance to the recent proliferation of info-snacking tools.

—letter to shareholders, April 18, 2008

The Evolution of Books

It's important to embrace new technologies instead of to fight them. You know, people forget the book itself is a technology and a very sophisticated one, and it's evolved from clay tablets, you know, to parchment and all kinds of things. You forget—because you're so accustomed to it, you forget that it's a technology.

—*Charlie Rose*, November 19, 2007

Books and Horses

I know over some time horizon, for sure, books will be read on electronic devices—you know, the vast majority will. I mean, you know, physical books won't completely go away just as, you know, horses haven't completely gone away.

—D: All Things Digital, May 27, 2008

●●●

The Purpose of the Amazon Book Store

If you come to the Amazon physical bookstore with a specific title in mind that you want to buy, there's a very good chance, because we have such a curated selection, that you'll be disappointed. . . . If you know exactly what you want to buy, we already have this thing called Amazon.com that's very, very good at satisfying that need. And so this is about satisfying a completely different need. It's about browsing and discovery and having a really fun space to wander around in.

—Code Conference, June 1, 2016

●●●

A Customer-Vetted Bookstore

We use the data from Amazon.com to curate that selection. So when you walk in there, almost every book in that store has 4.8 stars or more of customer reviews. And so it's kind of cool to walk around a store knowing that every book in the store has already been vetted by customers.

—*The Kindle Chronicles,* July 26, 2016

SPACE AND BLUE ORIGIN

....

To the Moon

It's time for America to go back to the moon, and this time to stay.

—Aviation Week's 60th Annual Space Laureate Awards, March 2, 2017

....

A New Golden Age of Space

I believe that we're entering a new golden age of space and space exploration, and that the time has come for that to happen because we as a species have upleveled ourselves in terms of technology. We're ready to do it now.

—John H. Glenn Lecture in Space History, June 14, 2016

•••

Earth Is the Best Planet

We will never find a place, in our solar system, anyway—probably never anywhere—that is as beautiful and comfortable as Earth. We evolved here—we've coevolved, actually, with this planet—and so it's kind of perfectly suited to us. But as we continue to expand we really need to go out into the solar system, and not just go to one planet or two planets but to go everywhere.

—Liberty Science Center Genius Gala 4.0,
May 1, 2015

•••

Use Space to Protect Earth

If you take baseline energy usage on Earth and grow it, compound it, at just 3 percent a year, such is the power of compounding that just in a few hundred years you'll have to cover the entire surface of the earth in solar cells to power the planet. . . . Ultimately, over the next few hundred years, we need to build a real spacefaring civilization. I think what's going to happen is we are going to move all heavy industry off Earth and we'll zone earth residential and light industrial. And we'll protect this glorious jewel of a planet because it is unique in our solar system, and we're unlikely to get to new solar systems any time soon.

—John H. Glenn Lecture in Space History,
June 14, 2016

I don't want a Plan B for Earth. I want Plan B to be make sure Plan A works. I think you go to space to save Earth.

—Code Conference, June 1, 2016

. . . .

Space or Stasis

Another route would just to be to face stasis and not continue to grow. I don't think that's as interesting. I don't think you want to just survive on this planet. I think you want, you know, to thrive and do amazing things. And to do that we need to go out into the solar system.

—Pathfinder Awards, October 22, 2016

It would be completely immoral of us to say, well, we'll just kind of freeze energy utilization where it is. Because the other 7 billion people who are just now coming online to more energy usage, they're going to want what we have.

—Code Conference, June 1, 2016

New Worlds Save Old Worlds

We are really evolved to be pioneers. For good reason. New worlds have a way of—you can't predict how or why or when—but new worlds have a way of saving old worlds. That's how it should be. We need the frontier. We need the people moving out into space.

—*Business Insider*, December 13, 2014

Entrepreneurship in Space

What I want to achieve with Blue Origin is to build the heavy-lifting infrastructure that allows for the kind of dynamic entrepreneurial explosion of thousands of companies in space that I have witnessed over the last 21 years on the internet.

—Vanity Fair New Establishment Summit,
October 20, 2016

Step by Step, Ferociously

Our motto at Blue Origin is "Gradatim Ferociter," which means "Step by step, ferociously." And what we want to do is first do this suborbital vehicle, and then we'll do, you know, a series of vehicles, and ultimately, the long-term goal is to be part of an industry that helps humanity get into space.

—BookExpo America, May 30, 2008

● ●

Blue Origin's Mascot

Our mascot is the tortoise because we believe slow is smooth and smooth is fast.

—Pathfinder Awards, October 22, 2016

● ●

Reusable Rockets

If you ask the question, "Why is space travel so expensive?" there is one reason, and it's because we throw the hardware away every time after using it.

—*Charlie Rose*, October 27, 2016

I think that, you know, space travel can be both much lower cost and much more reliable and safe. And, in fact, I think that reusability will add to reliability. . . . I would much rather fly a new Boeing 787 after it's been flying a little while and not like the very first flight out of the factory.

—John H. Glenn Lecture in Space History,
June 14, 2016

Rockets have always been expendable. Not anymore. Now safely tucked away at our launch site in West Texas is the rarest of beasts, a used rocket.

—Blue Origin blog, November 23, 2015

• •

New Shepard and New Glenn

We're working on two vehicles right now. One is called New Shepard. It's a suborbital tourism vehicle. It's named after the first American in space, whose name was Alan Shepard. We're working on a second vehicle, which is called New Glenn. It's named after John Glenn, the first American in orbit.

—opening of Apollo exhibit at the Museum of Flight,
May 20, 2017

• •

Democratizing Space Travel

The long-term goal of Blue Origin is to not only do suborbital, but also orbital, and to democratize space travel so that anybody who wants to go into space can afford to do so.

—AWS re: Invent, November 29, 2012

• •

The First Objective of Blue Origin

Our first objective is developing New Shepard, a vertical take-off, vertical-landing vehicle designed to take a small number of astronauts on a suborbital journey into space.

—Blue Origin blog, January 2, 2007

• •

The Purpose of New Glenn

We'll use [New Glenn] to do both commercial payload missions for satellite companies, and we'll use it to lift humans into space. And we'll be flying it by the end of this decade.

—Pathfinder Awards, October 22, 2016

• •

Advantages of New Shepard

One of the good things about this vehicle is it can fly autonomously. It's kind of a flying robot. It can fly itself up into space, bring itself back down, and land, so we don't have to put pilots at risk during the test program. And then, once we're completely confident in the vehicle, we'll start taking people up into space.

—*CBS This Morning*, November 24, 2015

• •

The BE-3 Engine

Liquid hydrogen is challenging, deep throttling is challenging, and reusability is challenging. This engine has all three. The rewards are highest performance, vertical landing even with a single-engine vehicle, and low cost.

—press release, April 7, 2015

••

Why Go to Space?

Those few people who have been lucky enough to go into space say that when you see the thin limn of the earth's atmosphere and see that view of the earth from space, that it does change you. It makes you recognize just how fragile and amazing this planet is. So we hope to be able to provide a lot of people with that experience.

—Aviation Week's 60th Annual Space Laureate
Awards, March 2, 2017

••

Space Tourism

I like tourism as a mission for spaceflight because the frequency of it can be very high, so you can do a lot of it. One of the things that we know is we humans get better at everything that we practice. And today the most-used launch vehicles only fly maybe a dozen times a year, and you just never get truly great at anything that you do only a dozen times a year.

—opening of Apollo exhibit at the Museum of Flight,
May 20, 2017

Space Training

It shouldn't be more than a day of training, and the system has been designed from the very beginning so that the training can be minimal. You have to know how to strap yourself in, among other things, but it's not a significant amount of training.

—Blue Origin press conference, April 5, 2017

A 21st-Century Booster Engine

We have tools and capabilities, software simulations, computational horsepower, that the builders of those great engines could have only dreamed about. We can build an engine today that is a 21st-century engine that has great reliability, low cost, low cost of operations, and high performance.

—Igniting the Future news conference,
September 20, 2014

Blue Origin and SpaceX

What SpaceX is trying to do is actually very similar, because the first stage of their orbital rocket is the only stage that they're trying to recover—and that first stage is suborbital. It's exactly like what we're doing.

—*CNN Money*, November 24, 2015

Elon Musk

We've talked to each other many times. And I think we're very like-minded about a lot of things. We're not twins in our conceptualization of the future or how space should develop. But there are a lot of similarities.

—*Florida Today*, March 12, 2016

Many Companies in Space

Space is so large that it can accommodate many winners. I hope SpaceX does well, Virgin Galactic too, and also others. Large industries are not made up of a single company, but of a multitude of companies, so an ecosystem can be created.

—*La Repubblica*, July 24, 2016

Making a Lunar Landing Happen

Our liquid hydrogen expertise and experience with precision vertical landing offer the fastest path to a lunar lander mission. I'm excited about this and am ready to invest my own money alongside NASA to make it happen.

—*Washington Post*, March 2, 2017

AI in Space

One of the things that artificial intelligence has in store for the future of space exploration, I believe, is just ever-better robotic probes to explore the solar system.

—opening of Apollo exhibit at the Museum of Flight,
May 20, 2017

F-1 Engine Recovery

A year or so ago, I started to wonder, with the right team of undersea pros, could we find and potentially recover the F-1 engines that started mankind's mission to the moon? I'm excited to report that, using state-of-the-art deep sea sonar, the team has found the Apollo 11 engines lying 14,000 feet below the surface, and we're making plans to attempt to raise one or more of them from the ocean floor.

—*Bezos Expeditions*, March 28, 2012

Space Resources

If you want to live in space for long periods of time and do so cost-effectively, you have to use the resources that you find in space.

—opening of Apollo exhibit at the Museum of Flight,
May 20, 2017

• •

Passion versus Business

When I started Blue Origin, which is the name of this space company, I did not make a list of all the businesses in the world where I thought I might get the highest return on invested capital. And it was driven by passion and curiosity and the need to explore the things that I care about.

—*Charlie Rose*, October 27, 2016

• •

How Much He's Invested in Blue Origin

Maybe one day I'll disclose the size of the investment, but probably not today. Let's just say it's a lot. And let's also say I feel incredibly fortunate that I'm able to afford this investment.

—*Ars Technica*, March 9, 2016

• •

Passion versus Business

My passion is for space, for sure. But I do think that this can be made into a viable business. I think you have to be very long-term oriented.

—*Charlie Rose*, November 19, 2007

Making the Impossible Possible

For a long time, many, I mean, hundreds of years, thousands of years, the idea of going to the moon was so impossible, that people actually used it as a metaphor for impossibility. And then, in the 1960s, we humans did it. And I would hope you would take away from that, is that anything you set your mind to, you can do. Von Braun said after the lunar landing, "I have learned to use the word 'impossible' with great caution."

—opening of Apollo exhibit at the Museum of Flight, May 20, 2017

INVESTMENTS AND PHILANTHROPY

• •

Investing in Curiosity

In my personal investments I'm mostly doing things that I'm curious about. And passionate about. In many cases I don't necessarily expect them to be good investments.

—*Telegraph*, August 16, 2015

• •

Buying the *Washington Post*

I bought it because it's important. I would never buy a financially upside-down salty snack food company. That doesn't make any sense to me. But the *Washington Post* is important.

—*Charlie Rose*, October 27, 2016

••

A Self-Sustaining Newspaper

This is not a . . . philanthropic endeavor. And the reason is, for me, I really believe that a healthy newspaper that has an independent newsroom should be self-sustaining. And I think it's achievable, and it is achievable.

—The Future of Newspapers, June 21, 2017

••

Constraints Drive Creativity

Constraints drive creativity. You know, the worst thing I could have done for the *Post*, I believe, is to have said, you know, don't worry about revenue, [have] whatever you need, just do the job. . . . I don't think that would lead to as much quality as you get when there are, in fact, constraints.

—The Future of Newspapers, June 21, 2017

••

Free Speech

We have fundamental laws and we have consitutional rights in this country to free speech, but that's not the whole reason that it works here. We also have cultural norms that support that, where you don't have to be afraid of retaliation. And those cultural norms are at least as important as the Constitution.

—The Washington Post's Transformers, May 18, 2016

The Importance of the *Washington Post*

The values of the *Post* do not need changing. The paper's duty will remain to its readers and not to the private interests of its owners. We will continue to follow the truth wherever it leads, and we'll work hard not to make mistakes. When we do, we will own up to them quickly and completely.

—*Washington Post*, August 5, 2013

Democracy dies in darkness. Certain institutions have a very important role in making sure that there is light, and I think the *Washington Post* has a seat, an important seat, to do that, because we happen to be located here in the capital city of the United States of America.

—The Washington Post's Transformers, May 18, 2016

Using Amazon's Approach at the *Washington Post*

We've had three big ideas at Amazon that we've stuck with for 18 years, and they're the reason we're successful: put the customer first. Invent. And be patient. If you replace "customer" with "reader," that approach, that point of view, can be successful at the *Post*, too.

—*Independent*, September 3, 2013

We attempt to be customer-centric, which in the case of the *Post* means reader-centric. . . . I think you can get confused. You can be advertiser-centric, and what advertisers want, of course, is readers. And so you should be simpleminded about that and you should be focused on readers. And if you can focus on readers, advertisers will come.

—The Future of Newspapers, June 21, 2017

• •

Making Money on the *Washington Post*

We have to go from a business model where we used to make a relatively large amount of money per reader with a relatively small number of readers to a model where we make a relatively small amount of money per reader but on a very large number of readers.

—Code Conference, June 1, 2016

• •

Luxury Newspapers

I think printed newspapers on actual paper may be a luxury item.

—*The Today Show*, September 25, 2013

••

The 10,000 Year Clock

We are building a 10,000 Year Clock. It's a special Clock, designed to be a symbol, an icon for long-term thinking. It's of monumental scale inside a mountain in West Texas. The father of the Clock is Danny Hillis. He's been thinking about and working on the Clock since 1989. He wanted to build a Clock that ticks once a year, where the century hand advances once every 100 years, and the cuckoo comes out on the millennium. The vision was, and still is, to build a Clock that will keep time for the next 10,000 years.

—10000YearClock.net, June 2011

You start thinking about things differently if you think in 10,000-year time horizons. We humans are now very capable of changing the planet in a bunch of ways, and because we've got so technologically capable as a species we need to think long-term, not just about climate and natural ecosystems, but about civilization and all kinds of things.

—*Metro*, October 15, 2012

● ●

Giving Money Well

We want to figure out how to do philanthropic work that's highly leveraged. It's very easy to give away money ineffectively. But doing it well requires at least as much attention and energy as building a successful company.

—*Time*, December 27, 1999

● ●

Short-Term Philanthropy

I'm thinking about a philanthropy strategy that is the opposite of how I mostly spend my time— working on the long term. For philanthropy, I find I'm drawn to the other end of the spectrum: the right now.

—Twitter, June 15, 2017

LIFE LESSONS

A Sense of Wonder

It's a gift if you can keep your childlike sense of wonder, and it helps with creativity. It helps to have fun. You know, you laugh more and play more if you keep that childlike sense of wonder.

—*Four Peaks*, September 13, 2013

Fundamental Goodness

It's impossible to interact with an eighteen-month-old child and not come away with the impression that people are fundamentally good.

—*Esquire*, January 29, 2007

Role Models

In life, we get a lot of rolls of the dice. One of the big rolls of the dice is who are your early role models, so I try to do that for my kids.

—*Business Insider*, December 13, 2014

••

Inspiring the Next Generation

I was inspired by invention and self-reliance from a number of different people and from, you know, even watching the Apollo program as a little boy. And I think when little kids get inspired, you never know what might happen.

—*Four Peaks*, September 13, 2013

••

Great Teachers

They create that environment where you can be very satisfied by the process of learning that's going on. It's like anything—if you do something and you find it to be a very satisfying experience, then you want to do more of it. And so the great teachers somehow convey, in their very attitude, and their words, and their actions, and everything they do, that this is an important thing you're learning.

—American Academy of Achievement interview,
May 4, 2001

••

Deferred Gratification

When you're young, deferring gratification is not a honed skill. As you get older, you get better at the marathon mentality.

—*Esquire*, January 29, 2007

Task-Switching

I've always been focused. When I was in Montessori school, the Montessori school teacher told my mom that I wouldn't switch tasks. And they got me to switch tasks by picking me up—including my chair—and just moving me to the new task station. I've gotten a little better about that over the years, but it's still—task-switching is still a problem for me.

—opening of Apollo exhibit at the Museum of Flight,
May 20, 2017

Your Passions Choose You

You don't get to choose your passions. Your passions choose you.

—*Business Insider*, December 13, 2014

Do something you're very passionate about. And don't try to chase what is kind of the hot passion of the day.

—American Academy of Achievement interview,
May 4, 2001

Many, many kids and many grown-ups do figure out over time what their passions are. . . . I don't think it's that hard. I think what happens, though, sometimes, is that we let our intellectual selves overrule those passions—and so that's what needs to be guarded against.

—*Four Peaks*, September 13, 2013

The Older You Get, the Less You Know

One of the things that it's very hard to believe when you're 22 or 23 years old is that you don't already know everything. It turns out, I mean, as I suspected, you know, people learn more and more as they get older, [but] that you seem to realize you know less and less every year that goes by. I can only imagine that by the time I'm, you know, 70, I will realize I know nothing.

—American Academy of Achievement interview,
May 4, 2001

First Jobs

The most important thing about your first job out of school is to pick a place where you think your learning per unit time is going to be very high.

—lecture to the MIT ACM/IEEE Club,
November 25, 2002

Anger

You should never counsel anger.

—Vanity Fair New Establishment Summit,
October 20, 2016

Gifts and Choices

Cleverness is a gift. Kindness is a choice. Gifts are easy. They're given, after all. Choices can be hard. You can seduce yourself with your gifts if you're not careful, and if you do, it will probably be to the detriment of your choices.

—Princeton University commencement address,
May 30, 2010

Be proud, not of your gifts, but of your hard work and your choices.

—opening of Apollo exhibit at the Museum of Flight,
May 20, 2017

The Regret Minimization Framework

The right framework, for me, anyway, to make the kind of decision was a regret minimization framework. So I projected myself into the future, and I'm 80 years old and I'm looking back on my life. What do I want to have done at that point? I want to have minimized all the regrets that I have. And I knew that when I was 80, there was no chance that I would regret having walked away from my 1994 Wall Street bonus or any of that kind of thing. I wouldn't even remember that. But I did think there was a chance that I might regret not having participated somehow in this thing that I thought was going to be very exciting called the internet.

—A.B. Dick Lecture on Entrepreneurship, March 21, 1998

Regrets of Omission, Not Commission

Most regrets, by the way, are acts of omission and not commission.

—American Academy of Achievement interview,
May 4, 2001

People Who Are Right

People who are right a lot, they listen a lot. And people who are right a lot change their mind a lot. And people who are right a lot, they seek to disconfirm their most profoundly held convictions.

—Pathfinder Awards, October 22, 2016

Changing Your Mind

I change my mind even when the data doesn't change . . . because I reanalyze the situation every day, and sometimes I just come to a better analysis and I think, actually, what I said yesterday I don't believe anymore, and we should change that.

—The Washington Post's Transformers, May 18, 2016

Conventional Wisdom

Conventional wisdom is usually right.

—Vanity Fair New Establishment Summit,
October 20, 2016

. . . .

Dealing with Stress

Stress primarily comes from not taking action over something that you can have some control over.

—American Academy of Achievement interview,
May 4, 2001

. . . .

The Key to Happiness

Eighty percent of your happiness depends on who you choose as your companion.

—*La Repubblica*, July 24, 2016

. . . .

His Wife

I think my wife is resourceful, smart, brainy, and hot, but I had the good fortune of having seen her résumé before I met her, so I knew exactly what her SATs were.

—*Vogue*, February 19, 2013

. . . .

Doing the Dishes

My wife still claims to still like me. I don't question her aggressively on that. I do the dishes every night, and I can see that actually makes her like me. It's a very odd thing.

—*Business Insider*, December 13, 2014

••

Lean In

I tell people, when the world changes around you, and it changes against you, so that what used to be a tailwind is all the sudden a headwind, you have to lean into that and figure out what to do. Because complaining is not a strategy.

—*ABC News*, September 25, 2013

••

Levered Time

We all have a limited amount of time, and where you spend it and how you spend it is just an incredibly levered way to think about the world.

—Ignition, December 2, 2014

A lot of people, and I'm just not one of them, believe that you should live for the now. I think what you do is you think about the great expanse of time ahead of you and try to make sure that you're planning for that in a way that's going to leave you ultimately satisfied.

—American Academy of Achievement interview, May 4, 2001

● ●

People Don't Change after Winning the Lottery

I think people overestimate the degree to which lottery winners' lives change. Certainly people at Amazon.com, including me, were a kind of lottery winner. But since people's personalities are largely set by the time they're 25, winning the lottery doesn't change them that much.

—Playboy, February 2000

● ●

Personal Time

It's easy to let the inbox side of your life overwhelm you, so you become a totally reactive person . . . The only remedy I know of is to set aside some fraction of your time as your own. I use Tuesdays and Thursdays as my proactive days, when I try not to schedule meetings. I let the other three days of the workweek be completely scheduled, meeting with different general managers in our businesses.

—Wall Street Journal, February 4, 2000

● ●

Planning

No plan survives its first encounter with reality.

—Time, December 27, 1999

••

The Pursuit of Happiness

I think sometimes, we as a society start to get confused and think that we have a right to happiness. But if you read the Declaration of Independence, it talks about life, liberty, and the pursuit of happiness. Nobody has a right to happiness. You should have a right to pursue it, and I think the core of that is liberty.

—American Academy of Achievement interview,
May 4, 2001

••

Get a Thick Skin

The best defense to speech that you don't like about yourself as a public figure is to develop a thick skin.

—Code Conference, June 1, 2016

••

Family Investment

I suspected that we would fail, and I told all of our early investors that they would lose their money for sure. This is—I think this is a good technique when you're taking money from friends and family, because you still want to be able to go to Thanksgiving dinner.

—Association of American Publishers,
March 18, 1999

What He Learned from His Helicopter Crash

I have to say, nothing extremely profound flashed through my head in those few seconds. My main thought was, This is such a silly way to die. It wasn't life-changing in any major way. I've learned a fairly tactical lesson from it, I'm afraid. The biggest takeaway is: Avoid helicopters whenever possible! They're not as reliable as fixed-wing aircraft.

—*Fast Company*, August 1, 2004

What Motivates Him

I have realized about myself that I'm very motivated by people counting on me. I like to be counted on. I like to have a bunch of customers who count on us. I like being part of a team. We're all counting on each other. I like the fact that shareholders are counting on us. And so I find that very motivating.

—*Fortune*, November 16, 2012

Work-Life Harmony

I think work-life harmony is a good framework. I prefer the word "harmony" to the word "balance" because balance tends to imply a strict tradeoff. In fact, if I'm happy at work, I'm better at home—a better husband and better father. And if I'm happy at home, I come into work more energized—a better employee and a better colleague.

—*Thrive Global*, November 30, 2016

MILESTONES

1964

- Jeff Bezos is born as Jeffrey Preston Jorgensen in Albuquerque, New Mexico, to Jackie and Ted Jorgensen.

1965

- Jackie files for divorce from Jorgensen.

1968

- Jackie marries Miguel Bezos. Miguel adopts Jeff, and the new family moves to Houston.

1969

- Bezos watches the televised Apollo 11 moon landing and resolves to go to space himself one day.

1977

- Bezos is featured in the book *Turning on Bright Minds: A Parent Looks at Gifted Education in Texas*.

1982

- Bezos graduates from Miami Palmetto Senior High School as valedictorian, a National Merit scholar, and the recipient of the prestigious Silver Knight award given by the *Miami Herald* to promising high school graduates. Bezos gives his valedictory speech on the importance of human colonization in space.

- Bezos begins attending Princeton University, initially majoring in physics. He later changes his major to computer science and electrical engineering after realizing he doesn't have the talent for physics that some of his fellow students do.

1986

- Bezos graduates Phi Beta Kappa from Princeton. After graduation, he begins working for Fitel, a Wall Street start-up that uses computer programming for financial communications.

1988

- Bezos begins working at Bankers Trust developing computer programming for banking client services.

1990

- Bezos is hired at D.E. Shaw, a hedge fund firm, as vice president.

1993

- Bezos marries MacKenzie Tuttle, a coworker at D.E. Shaw and fellow Princeton graduate.

1994

- Doing research at D.E. Shaw, Bezos realizes that the internet is growing at a rate of 2,300 percent a year. After some deliberation, he quits his job, raises money from angel investors (including $300,000 from his parents), hires employees, and moves to Seattle to start an internet commerce company selling books.
- Bezos incorporates the company as Cadabra but soon renames it Amazon.

1995

- Amazon launches in July out of the garage in Bezos's Bellevue, Washington, home. The first book it sells is *Fluid Concepts & Creative Analogies: Computer Models of the Fundamental Mechanisms of Thought*. Within two months, Amazon sells books to customers living in 50 states and 45 different countries.

1996

- Amazon launches its Associates program. The program allows third-party websites to earn money by linking to Amazon.

1997

- Barnes & Noble sues Amazon, arguing that its claims to be the "world's biggest bookstore" are false as Amazon is a broker and not a store. The lawsuit is settled out of court.

- Amazon goes public in May. Share prices are 30 percent higher than anticipated, and Amazon ends up raising $54 million, with a $430 million market valuation.

- Amazon introduces and patents the 1-Click method of shopping, which customers can use to purchase items with just one click.

1998

- Bezos invests $250,000 in Google.

- Amazon acquires the Internet Movie Database.

- Amazon begins to expand its product offerings, beginning with CDs and DVDs. Other new product categories systematically follow.

- The first international Amazon websites are launched in Germany and the United Kingdom.

- Walmart sues Amazon, claiming that the company has headhunted its executives and stolen secrets. The lawsuit is settled out of court.

1999

- *Barron's* nicknames the company "Amazon.bomb," predicting that the online retailer won't survive due to its low pricing strategy and expansion of its costly fulfillment infrastructure. A slew of critical articles and nicknames for the company follow.

- Amazon starts selling toys, games, and consumer electronics.

- Amazon sues Barnesandnoble.com for infringing on its patented 1-Click order technology.

- *Time* names Bezos its Person of the Year.

2000

- In March, market shares for tech companies reach their peak prices; over the next several years, the dotcom bubble bursts and most publicly traded dot-com companies—companies like Amazon—go under. While Amazon sees losses because of its heavy investments in online companies like Pets.com and Living.com, the retailer survives.

- Amazon's new logo, which has a smile spanning from A to Z, is first introduced in June.

- Amazon starts selling kitchen goods and cameras.

- Amazon partners with Toys "R" Us to become the toy retailer's exclusive online outlet, taking and fulfilling orders on the company's behalf. Several years later, the partnership ends in a lawsuit and dissension on both sides when Toys "R" Us wants to sell products on its own site and Amazon accuses the company of failing to maintain inventory.

- Amazon launches its retail marketplaces in France and Japan.
- Bezos founds spaceflight company Blue Origin in September but keeps its creation secret. Bezos funds Blue Origin by selling Amazon stock.
- After several failed attempts to compete with sites like eBay—including Amazon Auctions and zShops—Amazon launches Marketplace, its first successful third-party seller.

2001

- Amidst calls for profitability, Amazon fires 1,300 employees and reduces some customer service and fulfillment operations.
- Amazon partners with Borders and Target to sell their products via its own website.

2002

- Amazon begins its Free Super Saver Shipping program.
- Amazon and Barnesandnoble.com settle the suit over the patented 1-Click order technology.
- Amazon starts selling products in Canada.

2003

- Bezos begins buying extensive plots of land in West Texas in preparation for a Blue Origin testing facility.
- Amazon launches Amazon Services, which allows vendors to sell their goods on Amazon's website and use Amazon's fulfillment and customer service infrastructure to serve customers.
- A9.com, a search and mapping engine and subsidiary of Amazon, launches in October. The search engine fails to attract significant numbers of users and is gradually downsized.

- Bezos is involved in a helicopter accident on his property in West Texas. He is not seriously injured.
- Amazon makes its first full-year profit: $35.3 million.

2004

- Gregg Zehr founds Amazon Lab126, a research and development arm of Amazon which goes on to develop the Kindle e-reader, the Kindle Fire tablet, the Fire phone, the Echo, and the Echo Dot.
- Amazon acquires Chinese online retailer joyo.com in order to expand into the Chinese market.

2005

- Amazon Prime is introduced to customers in January, providing members free annual shipping for a $79 yearly flat rate.
- Bezos first announces his plans to develop a reusable suborbital space vehicle in an exclusive interview with West Texas newspaper the *Van Horn Advocate*.
- Blue Origin tests the Charon test vehicle, which is powered by jet engines. The launch is meant to test the vehicle's control guidance technologies in preparation for later space vehicle development.
- Amazon Mechanical Turk launches. Bezos calls it "artificial artificial intelligence." Users are paid very low wages to complete tasks that require human intelligence, such as transcribing PDFs or identifying objects in photographs.

2006

- Amazon Simple Storage Service begins renting Amazon's servers for file storage. This is the first introduction of a component of Amazon Web Services, a new division of Amazon that provides computing platforms to outside entities.

- Amazon introduces the Elastic Compute Cloud, which rents the data infrastructure that Amazon originally built for its own purposes out to developers. The Elastic Compute Cloud is a part of Amazon Web Services.

- Blue Origin tests the Goddard space vehicle.

- Fulfillment by Amazon launches, allowing third-party sellers to use Amazon's customer service system and store their goods in Amazon's distribution warehouses.

2007

- CreateSpace allows self-published authors to more easily print and distribute their books via Amazon.

- AmazonFresh, a grocery delivery service, begins with operations in Seattle.

- The Kindle, a dedicated e-reader and one of Amazon's first forays into hardware, launches in November after three years of development. The Kindle promises to deliver books within 60 seconds via wireless download. The device sells out in just over five hours.

2008

- Amazon buys audiobook vendor Audible for $300 million.

- Bezos is given an honorary doctorate in science and technology by Carnegie Mellon University.

- *Publishers Weekly* names Bezos its Person of the Year.

2009

- The Kindle 2 premieres with an easier-to-use layout and improved e-ink resolution. Later in the year Amazon also introduces Kindle DX, the first Kindle that allows users to read PDF documents.

- Amazon launches Amazon Publishing, a book-publishing component to the business. The publishing company is criticized in a 2014 *New Yorker* article for failing to generate revenue and attention.

- Amazon acquires Zappos, the online shoe retailer. Bezos explains that the purchase decision was made because of the two companies' shared value for customer service.

- Bezos receives the Henry Crown Leadership Award from the Aspen Institute.

2010

- Kindle apps that are rolled out in late 2009 and 2010 make the Kindle store and e-books available on Blackberries, PCs, Macs, iPads, and Androids.

- Blue Origin receives funding from NASA to support program development as part of the Commercial Crew Development (CCDev) program.

- Amazon introduces its third-generation Kindle, the Kindle Keyboard. The Kindle Keyboard is slightly smaller and has a better resolution display than previous generations of the Kindle.

- Amazon signs an exclusive e-book distribution deal with the Wylie Agency, effectively excluding traditional publishers from the production, distribution, and sale of digital titles Wylie represents.

- Bezos gives $100,000 to help defeat a Washington State initiative that would have levied an income tax on the state's wealthiest residents.

- Amazon Studios begins. The studio develops and distributes film and television.

2011

- Instant Video, formerly known as Amazon Video, is added to customers' Prime packages. Instant Video does not initially include any original content from Amazon.

- Blue Origin again receives funding from NASA, this time under the CCDev phase 2 program.

- E-books sold on the Kindle begin to outpace sales of physical books on Amazon.
- Bezos announces plans to invest in the 10,000-year clock, which would be built inside a mountain in West Texas and keep time for the next 10,000 years. Bezos calls it a symbol for long-term thinking.
- Bezos invests in Airbnb, a website that allows users to rent out rooms and homes to guests.
- Jeff and MacKenzie Bezos donate $10 million to the Museum of History and Industry in Seattle to establish the Bezos Center for Innovation, a permanent exhibit that showcases the spirit of invention in Seattle.
- The PM2 suborbital space vehicle flight test fails.
- The *Morning Call*, a local newspaper serving Lehigh Valley, Pennsylvania, reports on brutal working conditions in a nearby Amazon warehouse, where air conditioning had not been installed in the summer months and ambulances stayed in the parking lot to serve workers suffering from heat exhaustion.
- Kindle books become available for members of local libraries to rent on their devices.
- Amazon's first tablet, the Kindle Fire, is introduced.
- Amazon introduces the Kindle Touch, the first of its e-readers to use a touchscreen.
- Bezos and his wife MacKenzie donate $15 million to Princeton University to create the Bezos Center for Neural Dynamics, which will conduct cutting-edge brain research.
- Bezos invests in ride-share company Uber.
- The *Economist* gives Bezos and Gregg Zehr an Innovation Award in recognition of the Kindle.

2012

- Amazon Studios announces plans to begin developing original content for Amazon Instant Video.

- Bezos announces plans to recover the F-1 engine from the Apollo 11 spaceflight from the bottom of the ocean floor off the coast of Florida.

- Bezos is elected to the American Academy of Arts and Sciences.

- Jeff and MacKenzie Bezos donate $2.5 million to support a same-sex marriage referendum in their home state of Washington.

- The Kindle Paperwhite, which uses improved LED technology to improve the reading experience, enters the marketplace.

- Amazon acquires Kiva Systems, a company that uses robots to sort items in fulfillment centers. Kiva is later renamed Amazon Robotics.

- The Bezos Center for Innovation at the Museum of History and Industry in Seattle opens to the public.

- *Fortune* names Bezos its Businessperson of the Year.

2013

- Bezos and Amazon accept the National Retail Federation's award for Retailer of the Year.

- Amazon introduces AmazonSmile, which allows customers to opt in to a program that donates .5 percent of their Amazon purchases to a charity of their choice.

- The F-1 engine from the Apollo 11 expedition is successfully recovered off the coast of Florida.

- Amazon acquires Goodreads, a book review website.

- The Mayday button launches, giving near-instant tech support to users of devices like the Kindle Fire via a video connection to customer service representatives.

- Bezos purchases the *Washington Post* newspaper for $250 million.
- The research and development of Amazon drone delivery services is first announced to the public.

2014

- Amazon Fire TV allows streaming to TV.
- The International Trade Union Confederation names Bezos the World's Worst Boss.
- The Fire, Amazon's first smartphone, is introduced. The phone is a major flop, and Amazon cuts the price from $200 to 99 cents only a few months after it is first introduced.
- Amazon and book publisher Hachette engage in a lengthy public dispute over, among other things, e-book pricing. As a result of the conflict, according to Hachette, Amazon begins to place artificial delays on the delivery of the publisher's books to customers— what many publications see as a way for Amazon to bully Hachette into submission. By the end of the year they reach an agreement that allows Hachette to control prices for its own e-books and physical books and to reduce the share that Amazon receives from sales of books that Hachette itself had discounted.
- Amazon first announces the Echo and Alexa. Alexa is an artificially intelligent voice agent that powers the Echo, a home device. The Echo Dot, Amazon Tap (a portable version of the Echo), Echo Look (a camera with Alexa services built in), and Echo Show (which has an LCD screen) are introduced in the years to come.
- Blue Origin partners with United Launch Alliance to develop the BE-4, a rocket engine powered by liquid oxygen and liquefied natural gas.

- Prime Now service is announced and launched first in Manhattan. The shipping program, available only to Prime members, provides one-hour delivery in certain urban areas.

2015

- The Amazon Prime television show *Transparent* wins a Golden Globe for Best Television Series—Musical or Comedy, making it the first television program produced and distributed by a streaming-only service to win a Golden Globe for Best Series of any kind.

- In April, Blue Origin's suborbital launch vehicle New Shepard is tested for the first time.

- The Liberty Science Center grants Bezos a Genius Award.

- Amazon pledges up to $100 million to the Alexa Fund, which will invest in research and advancements in artificial intelligence technology.

- In July Amazon first introduces Prime Day, an Amazon promotion that gives Prime members exclusive deals over the course of a day.

- The *New York Times* publishes its exposé of Amazon's corporate workplace. The article includes interviews and testimonies from employees who say they were pushed out of their jobs for illness or pregnancy, as well as criticism of the company's brutal management style.

- Blue Origin announces that it will build new rocket manufacturing and launch facilities in Cape Canaveral, Florida.

- Amazon Restaurants, a restaurant delivery service, first launches in Seattle.

- Blue Origin announces plans to manufacture an orbital launch vehicle.

- In November, Blue Origin successfully launches the New Shepard into space and re-lands it on the launch pad.

- The first Amazon Books store—Amazon's first physical retail location of any kind—opens in Seattle.
- Amazon Studios releases its first feature-length film, Spike Lee's *Chi-Raq*.
- Bezos is ranked number one on *Fortune*'s list of World's Greatest Leaders.

2016

- Blue Origin tests the New Shepard again in January. It flies again three more times in 2016.
- Amazon releases the Kindle Oasis, which has several design functions to improve readability.
- Bezos is awarded the Pathfinder Award by the Museum of Flight in Seattle.
- Bezos wins the Heinlein Prize in recognition of his efforts to commercialize space exploration. He donates his $250,000 in winnings to the nonprofit group Students for the Exploration and Development of Space.
- Blue Origin breaks ground on its Florida rocket manufacturing facility.
- Bezos is added to the Defense Innovation Advisory Board, which will help guide the Pentagon as it attempts to adapt private-sector technology breakthroughs to government initiatives.
- Bezos makes a cameo appearance in the film *Star Trek Beyond*.
- Blue Origin announces the development of orbital space vehicle New Glenn.
- Bezos invests in Unity Biotechnology, a start-up that develops anti-aging therapies.
- Bezos wins an American Ingenuity Award from *Smithsonian* magazine.

- Along with Bill Gates, Jack Ma, and other investors, Bezos invests in Breakthrough Energy Ventures, a fund that supports the development of clean energy alternatives.

- Bezos, along with Larry Page, Sheryl Sandberg, and other prominent tech CEOs, participates in President-elect Donald Trump's tech summit at Trump Tower in New York City.

- Amazon announces its new Amazon Go system, a physical retail store concept which would automatically charge customers for any items they take out of the store. The first store opens in December in Seattle, but subsequent store openings are delayed due to technical difficulties.

- The first delivery by drone is completed in England.

2017

- Amazon announces its opposition to an executive order signed by Donald Trump that would restrict immigration access to the United States from seven Muslim-majority countries.

- Bezos buys the largest private property in Washington, DC, for $23 million. The Bezos family's new residence was formerly the home of a textile museum. The family also owns homes in Washington State, Beverly Hills, and New York City.

- Amazon Studios wins its first three Oscars, two for *Manchester by the Sea* and one for *The Salesman*.

- *Fast Company* ranks Amazon first on its list of World's Most Innovative Companies of 2017.

- The New Shepard team wins Aviation Week's 60th cAnnual Space Laureate Award.

- Bezos and Blue Origin are awarded with the Robert J. Collier Trophy for achievement in American aeronautics.

- Amazon acquires Souq.com, an online retailer in the Middle East.

- Bezos donates $1 million to the Reporters Committee for Freedom of the Press. Bezos has been increasingly vocal about freedom of speech and the press since purchasing the *Washington Post* and since the election of President Donald Trump.

- In June, President Donald Trump takes to Twitter to accuse Amazon of avoiding paying sales tax. Trump continues to criticize Amazon and Bezos on Twitter throughout the year. The initial accusation came as a result of a story published in the *Washington Post* exposing the false provenance of the *Time* magazine covers hanging in Trump's home.

- Amazon buys the Whole Foods grocery chain for $13.7 billion.

- Bezos wins the inaugural Buzz Aldrin Space Innovation Award.

- For a brief period in July, Bezos unseats Bill Gates as the world's richest person, boasting a net worth of $90.6 billion.

- Amazon reveals its Instant Pickup concept, which would allow customers to pick up their Amazon purchases from a locker within two minutes of ordering them. The concept is first unrolled on college campuses in Berkeley, Los Angeles, Columbus, Atlanta, and College Park, Maryland.